THE UNFOLLOW EFFECT

Intentional Living in a Digital Age

Emily Feldpausch

Copyright

Copyright © 2025 *by* **Emily Feldpausch**

All rights reserved. No part of this book may be reproduced in any form or by any means—whether electronic, digital, mechanical, or otherwise—without permission in writing from the publisher, except by a reviewer, who may quote brief passages in a review.

Cover design by **Jersey Mark**

Paperback **ISBN: 979-8-9943429-1-6**

To those who crave to make the world a better place by starting with themselves. And to Josh, Evan, and Andy, may their future be bright.

Acknowledgments

I am deeply grateful to the many sharers in the world—authors, researchers, and podcasters—whose ideas I have reflected on and learned from, and who inspired me to share my own. I am especially thankful for deep conversations with good friends, the insight and guidance of my parents and in-laws, and years of analyzing others with my siblings.

Special thanks to everyone who encouraged me along the way—by talking with me about my articles, letting me know they loved my blog, or simply asking about this project. Your words, each and every one of them, are what pushed me to share when it felt scary to.

I'm grateful to the editors who helped me clear away the cobwebs and bring this work into focus. In particular, thank you to Nicole Heggelund and Emily Gallinger for their contributions to the completion of this project. Emily, for our many conversations about life and technology—and for insisting that you "see this thing," which ultimately pushed me to the finish line. Nicole, for your thoughtful suggestions and your steady support from the very first blog post. Thank you to the friends who offered help and continued to show up—even when I had to disappear into this project for weeks at a time.

Finally, I am endlessly grateful for my husband, Nathan, and our children—for reminding me to take my time with projects like this so I don't miss life along the way, and for continually helping me grow and think in new and different ways.

Preface

A Season of Clarity

Life becomes profoundly satisfying when you put your efforts into creating your own way. More than five years have passed since I began practicing intentionality with technology. Shifting from a chaotic to peaceful coexistence with the digital world didn't happen quickly. When I slowed down the hectic pace of my life during summer break, I finally took time to reflect. Having that mental space is what finally led me to clarity. Summer is my jam. As a teacher, I am lucky to get a little break from work— what I like to call "practice retirement." In addition, I feel a sense of kinship with the sun and the sweat. It makes me feel carefree and hopeful. A June weekend in Northern Michigan helped me simplify what I'd been trying to do: *unfollow*. This was the first step I took. I soon adopted *unfollowing* as my mindset, and it became my defense against anything that didn't lead me to the fulfilling, authentic moments I wanted for my life. It was the key to lasting change. So far, I have yet to look back.

The idea to *unfollow* came to me in a light-bulb moment on a jet ski ride with my husband and two of our kids. I was free to receive in that moment because I was in the moment. It seems that's when profound thoughts come to us. I can't recall all the times I've been driving with some good tunes, or in the shower, or hanging with friends when thoughts light up in my mind. I frantically try to remember them long enough to write them down before I forget. The unfollow idea came to me as a solution to the long-term conflict I had been having with integrating social media and smartphones into my life. Then, without much effort, I had an entire notebook filled with thoughts. I was on a mission to solve the problem. *Unfollowing* meant that I was done following the norm. Specifically, I was done being on social media mindlessly at the cost of living my best life.

The verb *unfollow* meant something important to me as well: "to cease to track a person or a group on a social networking site."[1] There were some platforms I knew I would find valuable enough to keep active, but they had to be personalized to work for me. The action I knew that was best for me was to unfollow the newsfeeds. So that's exactly what I did. I knew that in keeping the platforms active, I could check on loved ones at any time. And in posting, I could give others the choice to view mine if they wanted.

I was minimizing to maximize. The unfollowing wasn't about shutting people out of my life. It was about maximizing the relationships that mattered to me. It was about improving the relationship I had with myself as well. My realization, or my admittance, that it was the constant newsfeed that was bringing me down was eye-opening. The noise, the overstimulation, and the abundance of thoughts that came with the posts and the photos had become too much. The way certain posts brought confusing thoughts about people I knew was unsettling. It also made me question my self-esteem. Using social media without filtering out the noise makes it hard to follow our own values and purpose. Posts on popular platforms seem to all blend together. Photos follow the trends. Maybe I'm just too stubborn to follow the status quo, or maybe I'm smarter than I think. But I know one thing for sure: Years have gone by, and fighting against the current has been nothing short of amazing.

TABLE OF CONTENTS

Introduction

"I Just Don't Like this Weirdo Aspect of the World"

My experimentation with social media follows the path of most people who watched it unfold in real time in the late nineties. It began with AOL email and Instant Messenger. Then I joined MySpace (in 2003) and Facebook (in 2004) along with the others. Right on track, I dropped MySpace and kept Facebook. Next was adding millions of photos to Facebook and organizing them into albums that displayed a life well-lived. I eagerly added old friends and shamelessly spied on exes. But one day it stopped being fun. However, it wasn't until years later that I took my first break from the platform.

Joining in on the social media craze was hard to avoid. It wasn't long before I felt it might not be for me. I pretended it was, though, ignoring my instincts so I could keep with the status quo. I promptly *followed* the tech habits of the majority: posting, liking, checking, staring, scrolling, stalking. Fearful my existence would be null if I didn't share my cool life experiences, I posted incessantly. It easily grew into a habit from the validation and dopamine boosts alone. The onset of Facebook is when my "research" actually began. I recall the moment I felt *affected* after being on these sites and wanted to know why. I'd often ask friends about their feelings toward social media. More often than not, we had similar annoyances and felt confusion regarding our draw toward it. Like many, in between feelings of guilt and missing out, I convinced myself that I needed to *be online.* In staying with the trends, I joined the next popular platform, Instagram, in 2010.

The natural progression was to *influence.* As a seasoned teacher, co-owner of a fitness center, singer, visual artist, and certifiable #fitmom, I at least felt credentialed for the role. I posted more often and displayed the things I did in shiny, perfected photos. Spending time doing this was the experience I needed to learn from. I quit pretty soon. Maybe I could have been successful with it, but it just felt wrong. Having to allocate so much time online didn't seem very *influence*-worthy. Inspiring others with a pretend-perfect life only took away from being present in my real one. It made me less of a parent, family member, and human being, in the *real* world. The trade-off didn't seem worth any success it might amount to. After a few trials to maintain a presence, I found that platform didn't work for me either.

Growing increasingly skeptical and wary, I bounced between platforms, searching for any value they could provide. But a visceral gloom came over me whenever I jumped online, and I knew it was time to rethink things. I'm not one to allow toxins in my life once I identify them as such. I don't give many chances to those who treat me badly, so I don't know why I went along as long as I did. I started writing to process the beef I had with the digital world in general. I created a blog so I could share my thoughts in a place on the Web where my words weren't measured with *likes*. Once I got started, I couldn't stop thinking and writing about how there had to be a better way to coexist with the digital world. My thoughts came so fast I could barely get them on the page.

My beef? Years ago, we were thrown into a virtual world and given no tools on how to navigate it. We blindly logged on once and never stopped. Introspection and common sense seemed to go out the window. Strength in numbers took over, as well as the age-old mindset: *If everyone else is doing it, I'm going to as well.* One day screens started ruling our days. We were made to run, jump, explore, and play but instead have grown comfortable staring, straining, and sitting. We all started acting, dressing, and living eerily similar to one another. Many, especially young people, started feeling general malaise. Why wouldn't we? With FOMO, eye strain, and daily social comparison a daily companion, we didn't stand a chance. We unwittingly take on the habits of others that don't serve us or, even worse, impact us negatively. I'm just not following why we engage in a virtual world so wholeheartedly.

In observing the world around me, I started to see how we take little notice of the bad habits we're instilling into children. We are increasingly neglecting the earth we stand on and the people right in front of us. We call photos of our acquaintances making dinner a "newsfeed" and don't blink an eye at people around us staring 24/7 at a *thing* we ironically call a smartphone. A *thing* that infants today no doubt believe their parents love as much as them, if not more. A *thing* I both love and truly hate. The parent and the educator in me became worried, almost compulsively, about the negative repercussions from careless use of technology.

Peter Attia, M.D., in his book *Outlive*, said, "Medicine's biggest failing is in attempting to treat all these conditions at the wrong end of the timescale (after they are entrenched) rather than before they take root. As a result, we ignore important warning signs and miss opportunities to intervene at a point where we still have a chance to beat back these diseases, improve health, and potentially extend lifespan."[1] I couldn't help but connect this to the importance of paying attention to warning signs, and actual research, when it comes to using technology. I knew this was the time to follow my instincts when they told me to intervene, even when it was uncomfortable to go against the norm.

I started asking questions, observing myself and others without judgment, and researching. This book is my acceptance, or rather my *admittance*, that coexisting with the entire world on a computer screen bothers me. It is the process of working through that annoyance by learning from what others are doing right, and what we are doing wrong. It is the process of taking what I'm learning to create new rules, habits, and practices to live by. To make it official, I wrote a letter:

Dear Social Media,

I'm coming clean. It's not you, it's me. You know how they say a relationship should have more good days than bad? Well, ours has been bothering me for a while now. So it's time I take a step back.

Best regards,

Emily

I gave up any final efforts to follow along, or to pretend I was content in engaging the same way others were. I began a personal case study to find a way that I could use technology but not let it use me. I knew that the digital world was here to stay. I didn't want to delete or ignore everything but use technology in a healthier way. People will always post. Many will love it, and I will always like it *a little*. Overall, there are parts of it that can add value to my life and parts that I knew if I let go, my life would improve.

Blindly following along and joining in the social media craze was jeopardizing my own happiness. Drew Barrymore, in an interview about why she wasn't on social media, mirrored how I was feeling: "I just don't like this compulsive, instantaneous, over-information, lack-of-privacy, weirdo aspect of the world."[2] Feeling validated, I used Drew's words as my mantra: *I just don't like this weirdo aspect of the world*. They would pop into my head every time I compulsively scrolled through social media. I had reasons for not liking it. I was an introvert electing to do more socializing than the real world already provided. I already had dozens of hobbies, a great fitness and nutrition routine, spent time with friends and family, and was raising three active boys, but now I had this additional world to be in. I've never enjoyed watching reality TV, yet in scrolling the newsfeeds, I was electing to watch snippets of reality via video clips and photos.

Other technologies other than social media sometimes hindered my contentment as well. In addition to managing three email accounts, I was managing text messages minute by minute. I was even paying to store my digital clutter! Seeing what others were purchasing online increased how much I spent and decreased how good I felt about myself and others. A smartphone at my fingertips made me good at multitasking and bad at being present with the people in front of me. Balancing a real world with a virtual one made me say yes to things, even when my insides were screaming no!

So no, I don't really like the all-consuming digital aspect of the world. But I know as well as the next person that I have to learn to live with it. I let my life get out of hand because of technology. Identifying that was the first phase. My next one would be to make life good in spite of it. My goal was to have a smartphone, a television, video games, and a laptop but still put life and people first. I was hopeful a final phase could be to make life even better with the use of technology. As a business owner and writer, it could certainly add to those things, so long as I left the riffraff out.

I gained strength for my mission when I found myself having the same conversations with various peer groups. Others were also questioning what was happening in society today and felt they were mindlessly following along without any sense of how to use their values as a guide. I started to learn from those who were living the way I wanted to and to distance myself from the influence of those who weren't. Once I started working to find a solution, anything I read or researched about self-improvement easily applied to this "problem" I wanted to solve.

There are people who are unfazed by the screen, and those who happily coexist with it. But there are others like me, who are overwhelmed, fatigued, and increasingly discontent. If you are content as is, then you are lucky. If you are like me, then buckle down because we're going to do some work. This book is a collection of thoughts, wonderings, and ideas for better screen-life balance. It is my process for removing the excess in order to focus on the good stuff. It's about being intentional with the way I will and won't spend my time. In identifying what's working and what's not, I have figured out better habits, rules, and nonnegotiables. I now use technology so that it doesn't use me. If you have decided it's best to *unfollow* the way things are currently going and to work toward something different, let me be your guide.

Chapter 1

Unfollow Distractions from Real Life

We can't be online and be somewhere else too.

My initial reaction from my first social media break was that of a deep, cleansing breath. The kids and I left for a picnic at eleven o'clock without a phone or watch, and we didn't make it back home until four hours later. Since I didn't need my phone to take photos or check *like* updates, I didn't bring it. Taking those extra tasks off my back put my boys and me at ease. Only one day into the experiment, and I was sold. This first step gifted me a rare feeling of contentment. Leaving the phone at home allowed me to focus on playing an evil butterfly fighting against Spider-Man and his scary shark sidekick. Hearing my oldest giggle at my flying evil butterfly made me so happy. I regretted that we didn't always have such organic interactions. As they continued to run around, I sat several feet away. Not scrolling online or snapping photos allowed me to breathe, take in the moment, and really see them. Man are they cute when they're not fighting.

I'm not exaggerating when I say that sitting in the shade of a maple tree in a playground parking lot became one of my favorite moments as a parent so far. The rare stillness allowed me to meditate. I felt true contentment as my boys did their own form of meditation in the sandbox. The feeling beat out fun days at water parks, holiday celebrations, and even Disney Land. It was a mere four minutes before the moment was up, interrupted by my youngest who demanded I sprint around the parking lot with him. I enthusiastically joined in, but only one week earlier I would've said, "Hold on! After I post this video," or "Only if you smile one more time for the camera. Wait . . . one more." Four minutes was enough to create a forever memory—a mental photo to view at any time. It was enough to confirm I was heading in the right direction.

Committing to not using social media platforms for an unspecified time opened my eyes to how much the screen had been ruling my days. Being all-in on various platforms meant my phone was a crucial companion no matter where I went. It felt illogically wrong to do something cool and not immediately alert the media. Public documentation of daily life is how everyone is living these days, so it's easy to follow suit. Only in breaking from it can you determine if it is something worth living.

I am a curious observer of people in this digital age. My nineties self would be so confused—watching us literally pause what we're doing to browse through someone's digital photo albums, home videos, and diaries. I mean, Aunt Jane's photo album of Alaska was cool and all, but back then I wouldn't have pulled it out in the middle of dinner with friends. Middle-aged couples stare at phones as they wait for their meals. High school students feign attention during class. Elementary students relate everything back to *Minecraft or Roblox.* My grown adult peers (meant to be older and wiser) hypnotically gaze at bright little boxes no matter the event. People everywhere, big and small, pause tiny moments of life to tend to a glowing screen.

I am far less curious and way more critical when I observe myself. While all-in on social media, I caught myself acting less than ideal one too many times. I was short with my boys (ages four, three and one) if they interrupted my crafting of witty posts. I pretended to listen while compulsively checking who viewed my posts. I shared photos online of my boys without considering their privacy. The imbalance I started to observe in my own life led me to that first experiment.

That first break from social media put me on a learner's high. It motivated me to seek out other moments I might be unknowingly sabotaging. Vacations and concerts came to mind—experiences I can confidently say were more thoroughly enjoyed pre-smartphones and social media. I consider myself lucky to have traveled through Western Europe before the digital age.

Twenty-two and fresh out of college, I was a prime candidate for virtual distraction. Digital cameras and social media exploded into popularity just four months upon my return. They *just* missed me.

Back then it was true *vacating* from everyday life. Documenting a trip was writing words on paper and snapping one or two photos that *might be okay*. Without GPS we discovered hidden places when we inevitably got lost. There was no calling home until you reached a pay phone or a hotel. Only close friends knew where you were and when you would return. You simply disappeared from other friends and acquaintances for a while. The focus was on gazing at marvelous sights and meeting new people. It wasn't on capturing enough photos or on how many *likes* or *views* were being collected while trekking along. The experience of a concert distraction-free is indescribable. Without the option to share videos, there was freedom to truly immerse oneself in the music. People-watching and interacting with other fans were pleasant distractions as you anticipated the headliner's appearance.

These types of experiences changed when smartphones took off. They command we snap thirty photos on the coast of somewhere beautiful instead of trusting that relishing in the sunset glow is enough. They encourage us to spend minutes perfecting the chin-down-head-tilt-hand-on-hip stance and choosing the best filter. They nag us to take and post videos and check who *liked* it in the middle of a live performance of our favorite song.

I miss the good ole days when phones hung on the wall and not at our hips. I'd take wrangling a cord through the house any day over being tethered to a phone. We miss important interactions when we scroll and interact online, as opposed to when we are with others in person. Instead of providing escapism, experiences became the setting for personal reality TV shows. With no limit to how many photos that can be taken, there became pressure to take dozens under the guise of "preserving memories." Then photos started being taken for more than just memories because they provided virtual attention. It seems to have become more important to display that we're having a good time than to actually be having a good time. A successful experience is now measured by how many people *viewed* that we're doing something fabulous. If friends, family, acquaintances, and strangers don't validate how wonderful, cultured, and lucky we are, our experience can feel like a failure.

However, the true failure is in not being present in moments both big and small. They are being lost for the sake of multitasking with virtual interactions and presenting an ideal version of ourselves online. If we are stuck inside the virtual world while out with friends, on a beach, or even in a classroom, are we really existing in any of those spaces, with any of those in front of us? Many of us (namely Baby Boomers and Gen X) have an ability that, sadly, young people today do not. We can look back on memories devoid of a screen. We can look back on these to gain inspiration for bringing some of the magic back.

PROTECT SIMPLICITY:

- ***Don't take a photo at every occasion.*** I've always loved taking photos. It's not only fun, it also silences my fears. I believed that if I didn't take a photo, the memory would be lost. Because of this, I have hordes of printed photos stored in boxes in various closets and tucked away in cabinets. However, they have nothing on the tens of thousands of digital photos I have spread throughout my virtual spaces. This leaves me stressed more than full of glee when I look through them. With today's ability to take endless photos, instilling our own limits removes our attention from the screen and back to the moment. I took the leap and stopped taking photos at every occasion. In doing so, I realized there is nothing to fear. In fact, I've found there's much more to enjoy. And if fear of memories lost sets in, I look to the others in the group to share their photos and choose only a select few.

- ***If an event is deemed photo- or share-worthy, take pics at the start, then get fully into the moment.*** When I take footage of an event, I no longer strive for a perfect shot. I most often take it right in the beginning so that I can get that task over with and enjoy the event. If it is something I want to share with others, I wait until after the event to do so. This allows me to get a little documentation in before I immerse myself in having a great time.

- ***Let people know when you will be unavailable.*** Before smartphones, when we were off somewhere, we were just gone. We didn't get back to checking in with others until we got back to our house phones. Today, there is pressure to respond to others even when we are otherwise engaged. They know we have our phone on us. It feels like rejection when we don't respond. But many times, it feels like work to constantly respond. Responding to message after message certainly impacts how "in the moment" we can be. There are a couple of ways we can communicate we are off doing something else. Use the "notifications are turned off" message, for example. However, I feel texting a specific response could spread more intentionality, such as, "I will respond later. I'm at my child's baseball game right now." This clearly gets the point across and implies, *I am off living life. I am not responding to your message now.*

- ***Increase the distance between yourself and your phone whenever possible.*** Leave your phone in another room, turn it off, and leave your phone at home more often than not. Anything you can do that increases the effort to access your phone will condition you to stop checking. It is liberating to leave the ole ball and chain at home. I don't have a smartwatch to bring along either, so when I leave the phone behind, I am truly disconnected. There is freedom and fun in a trip to the grocery store without it, a walk to the park, or a dinner with friends. It gives me and those I'm with deserved undivided attention.

- ***Don't over-schedule.*** Being online can tempt you to sign up for everything under the sun. Highlight reels can make you believe you should be friending, or parenting, the way others are. But every activity I sign my kids up for is time away from the simplicity of just being with family. My spouse and I strive not to over-schedule our kids with play dates and structured activities, allowing them to have time to be present with us. While boredom may not always be enjoyable, I believe time at home together is essential for maintaining close family bonds.

- ***Turn off notifications from nonessential apps.*** Are minute-by-minute notifications from companies worth interrupting your time for? Do you really need to see dozens of alerts that a new color dropped at The Gap, or a new pizza is trending at Pizza Hut? I don't think so. Turn off automated notifications that are designed to distract. Turning on "focus mode" on your smartphone allows you to tailor it to allow messages from important people if needed.

- ***Don't check your phone first thing in the morning.*** Don't immediately lose the day by scrolling on your phone. Use that time to journal, read, or practice breathing or mindful meditation. Walk outside or leave the house, even if for a few minutes, before scrolling is allowed.

Chapter 2

Unfollow Scrolling-Induced Depression

At its best [Facebook] pacified me, at its worst it ruined my day.
—Ryan Nicodemus, The Minimalists

It only took one doom-scroll session to decimate my afternoon. I sat down on our beautiful covered patio on a seventy-degree day—a rarity in Michigan. I was planning on diving into a book, but I chose the phone instead. I went to check a simple thing on Facebook, probably details on an event, but instead I spent forty-five minutes scrolling through the pages of ambiguous highlights of the lives of others. On another occasion, I clicked on an old Instagram account I had created years ago but had forgotten about. This old one had not yet been minimized to following little, to no one, but was instead full of anyone the old me had decided to follow. In a matter of seconds, I was thrown a feed of best shots of everyone's vacations and perfected selfies. It was an accident I couldn't look away from. After twenty minutes of scrolling, I managed to peel myself away. I felt like a true victim of doom scrolling. Overwhelmed with guilt and confusion, I vowed to never succumb again.

If I said a long scroll only *occasionally* derailed my afternoon, it would be the understatement of the century. Almost every time I opened an app and scrolled through a feed of highlights, I felt crummy afterward. At the risk of sounding dramatic, many hours of my life were often ruined. I was doomed from the start of social media. My first feeling of FOMO was before it was a silly, overused term. Its use as a well-known acronym is comforting now because it removes the isolating feeling it caused me in the past. FOMO is what kept me engaging on social media, even though I didn't want to be on it. I did the dance for a while. A constant back and forth motion to find where I fit in with the virtual world. *Do I fully engage on the popular social media platforms? Do I simply post? Just scroll? Or should I cut it out completely?* I didn't want to be like others, content to give in to the urge to check out for thirty minutes here, fifteen minutes there. As someone prone to depression, I believe that social media and I perhaps don't mesh well together.

In reading *Feeling Good* by psychologist David D. Burns, I learned that many individuals who experience depression demonstrate distorted thinking, or negative thought patterns. We internalize the world and ourselves with negative thoughts. They are indestructible until identified and then trained to go away via cognitive behavioral therapy.[1] I've learned that sometimes a depressive feeling just arrives (aka a chemical cause). Perhaps from lack of sunlight in the winter, hormonal changes, or just our brain's makeup. Perhaps it's situational; something bad happens.

The last decade and a half has given me much to observe about depression. In my experience as an educator, fitness center owner, and parent, I witness various challenges people face in their daily lives. Depression was, of course, a certifiable condition before social media gave it more attention. But in the '90s, the most I remember connecting depression to was Kurt Cobain, Gothic clothing, and emotional lyrics. Today, my high school students readily admit their struggles with depression. It comes up regularly on popular social media feeds. It's mentioned in casual conversation. I was at a BBQ recently, and one of my friends casually referenced her depression. Out of a group of eight, seven of us elected to share that we related to her feelings. Depression seems to be more prevalent today than in the past.

This observation left me with a few questions. Does depression just *appear* more abundant because social media has opened the door to talk about it? Does scrolling cause depression? Are people experiencing *bad feelings* that mimic depression after too much time online? Or have we just lost an ability to process feelings in a healthy way? On one hand, some platforms can be a tool for outreach. On the other, culprits such as *likes*, FOMO, and social comparison seem to hardly cover the positives. I experience the negative side after an unfiltered scroll, but I also observe others who seem *unfazed.* Our minds must surely experience the virtual world differently depending on who we are.

My go-to thought patterns, engrained in me from a young age, were negative, and I was determined to combat how I responded to things years before the social media *craze* flooded the world. With the advice of a skilled therapist, I went all-in on psychologist David D. Burns's cognitive behavioral therapy strategy to *untwist* negative thought patterns. The Acceptance Paradox, a type of untwisting, worked wonders for me. Burns said, "Instead of defending yourself against your own self-criticisms, you don't try to build yourself up or fight back. Instead, you do just the opposite: You simply accept the fact that you are broken, imperfect, and defective. You accept your shortcomings with honesty and inner peace."[2]

I almost had it down: full acceptance of my flawed-self. Things that had ailed me for years were now no bother to me. I even got good at preparing for situations that awakened negative thoughts. I was pretty much "cured." That is, until the virtual world reared its ugly head. Though the depression was tamed, it was still on edge, ready to be provoked. Social media seemed to awaken the destructive thought tendencies I had worked so hard to erase. It only took engaging with a few popular platforms before I knew something was off. Facebook generally made me feel *bad*. Therefore, I left it and felt like my social life had survived. But feelings of guilt and missing out commanded I *be online*. Hence, I moved on to the next platform: Instagram. At first, I thought Instagram was making me happy. It was less *noisy* and more like the creative outlet I craved. It sucked me in, and my need for expression fast-forwarded into an attempt as an influencer. I was reinforced with a ping of joy every time I received a notification. Then I noticed the costs. The first price to this perceived joy was time. It meant liking and posting to no end. It meant crafting exemplary photos and pairing them with short, clever captions. The second price was mental fallout in earning less-than-stellar reviews on any post. It awakened familiar feelings, leaving me feeling *instabad*.

Even though I had the toolbox of strategies, applying them to the virtual world proved much more onerous. Just a five-second scroll did not give my brain a chance to counteract the *bad* thoughts, shifting my mood from neutral to irritated in 0.6 seconds. When my depressive moments were chemically based, perhaps I could've mustered through those bad feelings faster had I not decided to spend my free time online searching for justification that I should rightfully be depressed. Social media was *the* hotspot in my misery's search for company. I hypothesized that our minds naturally gravitate toward online noise that validates what we are most sensitive about. A social media newsfeed is on constant standby with a plethora of stimuli ready to confirm whatever negative thoughts lay dormant in my mind. My thoughts could not easily be "untwisted" because there was simply too much variety of hard evidence.

When thrown stimuli from social media, thoughts of self-acceptance were nowhere to be found. I personally stand unaffected by divisive political posts and photos of travel on the coast of some beautiful country. My mind fixates on inadequacies unique to me. When I was discontent with my social life, large neon signs of those with better friendships vied for my attention. A quick scroll revealed if they didn't invite me, or when I wasn't tagged for *National Friends Day.* The calming phrase "I accept my inadequacies without judgement" was no match to the love bombing of social media, with its intermittent dopamine hits. My brain preferred the stimulating, swirling vortex of engaging images and negative feelings over rational thinking. If the newsfeed did not give me enough, checking the status of likes on my own posts as compared to others gave me much more to work with. It was all solid confirmation that I am flawed, and without acceptance of this, my value is dependent on external stimuli—and that is a good way to become depressed.

Social media likes became a measure of self-worth. They were an easy way to gain approval or disapproval of who I presented online. The virtual collection of old friends, new friends, and acquaintances took on the job of quantifying my value. Checking the notifications on something I put out to the virtual world could make or break me. It was one thing to post advertisements about our small business and not get likes. But failing to get a hundred likes for a post that felt so open and honest was another. When I did not earn enough likes, or from whom I wanted them, it left me cleaning up the mess of my ruminating thoughts. Thoughts that whispered, *You are not worth others taking the time to double tap their screens.*

Even in knowing all the factors that play a role in engagement, I still let things like the quantity of likes determine how I felt about myself. Though I had mastered self-acceptance in real life, accepting my shortcomings, I didn't like seeing them in scroll form. I found myself back at square one. I had a decision to make. Should I continue the dance or quit it altogether? Was being online important enough to take the time to figure out how to live with it? Was it even possible to shush the thoughts and will myself to experience online life like everyone else? I knew that to maintain a social media presence, I would have to do the work to prevent the noise and the likes from reigniting my negative thought patterns. But the amount of time the processing of these thoughts took away from my family was alarming. So, I quit the dance. When it comes to social media, I follow my own social norms. In order to get the benefits from the parts I like, I unfollow, mute, delete, and post as I personally see fit. And until I deem it worthy of retraining my brain to function fully in the virtual world, I focus my energy on the real one I live and breathe in. I have a million-plus-one better things I can do instead.

PROTECT SIMPLICITY:

- ***Unfollow on social media platforms.*** On Facebook and Instagram, I keep people and pages I want to keep, but set them to *unfollow* mode so I can scroll through them when I feel it necessary. It gives me the ability to use the apps for specific purposes with less derailment. I learned that I could use social media if the accounts were set up this way because if I did fall back into old habits, then at least I would not see everyone's life highlights at all hours of the day. Instead, I'm seeing them when I choose to click on their page.

- ***Keep social media apps off your phone***. I had reasons for keeping an account on Facebook and Instagram. I didn't, however, have a need to be on them every day. Removing the apps from my phone takes away the compulsion to hop on there without good reason. Overstimulation from compulsively clicking on apps can mess with our dopamine levels, wreaking havoc on our mental health. Having to access the platforms through the browser helps me intentionally head to the platform for occasional, specific purposes. In the case that your smartphone adds the social media platform to your favorites, be careful to remove it.

- ***Practice self-acceptance.*** The practice of self-acceptance helps banish the nasty thief of joy: comparison. Comparing ourselves to others leads to a dead end. It's like comparing apples to oranges. Only by accepting who we are, shortcomings and all, can we free ourselves to accept our uniqueness.

- ***Look through your own highlights***. Many of us are in the habit of looking through the virtual photo albums of others and are neglecting our own. My enjoyment of what I post is limited due to the nature of outsiders viewing my personal moments as well. Therefore, having alternate means of viewing my own photos and personal achievements is a priority for me. Whether by creating a private Instagram account, curating a digital collection, using a digital photo frame, or printing photos and awards, find a way to keep some memories sacred. Two of the most joyful people I've known, my spouse's grandparents, had their entire refrigerator covered in family photos. Taking the time to

view your own photos, rather than always looking at others'
is a good way to practice gratitude and to limit comparison.

- ***Dish out self-love***. Look yourself in the mirror and speak affirming words. Practicing this form of self-love instead of getting on your phone can go a long way. There's also the High 5 Habit that was made popular by Mel Robbins where she states giving yourself a high-five in the mirror boosts your confidence and mental well-being.[3]

- **Hide like counts.** Until social media platforms decide to remove this feature, hiding the ability to instantly see your *likes*, and the *like* counts of others, is the next best thing. This allows you to look through your content, and the content of others, with less distraction.

- ***Set aside specific time for social media***. Sporadically popping onto them has hidden impacts. Before I was intentional with when I would check social media, I felt a depletion of good feelings. One-on-one time with a friend, good conversations, engagement with loved ones, and continual learning all fill my bucket with love and contentment. Scrolling after a good time made me forget about the one I just had and forced me to compare my life to others' highlights. The feeling can best be described as a spilling of that bucket. Being deliberate with when I check social media helps prevent that from happening.

Chapter 3

Unfollow Neglecting Your Personal Values

Remain true to your values. If you don't stand for something,
you'll fall for anything.

—Frank Sonnenberg

I kept a journal my whole childhood and well into my twenties. I went through the progression of keeping a diary, one that my brother stole from me a time or two to torment me on the contents of who I was crushing on in my pre-teens, to journaling in an attempt to process through boyfriends from junior high and beyond. I evolved to travel journaling and wrote detailed accounts of my adventures. The practice came to a stop with the arrival of the digital age. But then the pandemic started. When others tuned more into their screens, I felt drawn back to pencil and paper. It felt like both therapy and a mission. I integrated technology and shared it as a blog. In the midst of the pandemic, it felt especially important to highlight mental illness. After all, how could the diagnoses of mental illness not have increased from social media use when we were all staring at the screen a thousand times more than we did before? I thought others could find inspiration to improve their own relationship with social media too. The mission started off strong, but as I grew a following I struggled. I began writing to that audience instead of staying true to who I was. I started to fear sharing my authentic self. I questioned why I was sharing my writing at all.

American naturalist and essayist Henry David Thoreau's writings never cease to empower me. They encourage me to continue to share my thoughts. Thoreau wasn't one to follow the masses. He could have simply lived the unconventional life of solitude he preached, never to share a word about what he learned. His influence still reaches people today. There is a lot of value in sticking to your guns. It can feel lonely at first, but your personal values can guide you to a fulfilling life. Taking the time to identify my personal values has helped me understand why I have my convictions in this digital age. Staying true to my values helps me coexist with digital media in ways that optimize my life. It enabled me to find joy in being social in the virtual world. I was pretty content with a simple no-social-media presence for a portion of my life. Then my husband and I started various ventures – a fitness business, a blog, a family. When it comes to the business, we actually do very well with word-of-mouth advertisement. Yet it's undeniable that a business really shouldn't ignore the benefits of having an online presence. In learning that blogging is not simply writing but also requires some engaging online, I had a decision to make. I could keep my thoughts hidden or I could meet people where they are at to share them. I was challenged by the idea that some topics are too important not to talk openly about, embarrassing or not. I decided to keep working to share them. With kids, I don't feel that I owe anyone anything regarding the posting of their achievements and activities. We see a lot of our family, immediate and extended, pretty often.

However, I struggle with not sharing their beautiful moments with others. I want to engage with the social part of the virtual world while carefully maintaining a positive relationship with it.

The realization I had was that my use of digital media has to be in alignment with my values. I knew that certain social media platforms would be the most efficient way to keep in alignment with them. However, somewhere between running a business, teaching, and being a wife and mother, I had completely lost sight of what my values actually were. How could I be my best self in the "real world," let alone the virtual one, if I hadn't honestly identified those values? Once I sat down and thought about it, my values were brought to the forefront. Identifying values can be a little daunting. There are plenty of books and resources for help with figuring them out. As a start, I identified some nonnegotiables for my life and what I wanted to drive my everyday actions.

Honesty

I had done my share of lying in my early dating years. I had also done more than my share of people-pleasing in which I lied about wanting to do certain things for others. One day I decided that I wouldn't lie anymore, and my "real life" has been wonderfully simple ever since. The awakening of social media is when things got dicey. When I was all-in on Instagram, many times I felt out of alignment simply by posting photos and captions of me appearing to have it altogether when, in fact, it couldn't have been further than the truth. Another part of being honest in this digital age is not *liking* or responding to a plethora of notifications throughout the day simply to appease others.

Spreading Kindness

A united community is an aspect that we all love about social media. We're made aware of GoFundMe pages. It allows us to give shout-outs. We often see supportive statements such as, "You're beautiful!" or "Keep up the good work!" But for me, any kindness that spreads on social media only adds to its addictive nature. At first, it went against my kind nature to stop supporting people online, but I found in putting my efforts outside the screen, I forgot all about that notion.

Love Without Agenda . . . Like a Child

I remember when I started saying "I love you" to family and friends. It wasn't really something my family did growing up. One day when I was a little older, it naturally came forth and clicked. I attempt to show love not just in words but in actions as well. And I try and show it like a child without agenda and without thought. There came a point where I realized I was caught in a web of sharing love online for selfish reasons. "A like for a like" in a sense. Identifying that flaw helped me make decisions on how to spend my time. I made the decision to choose social media platforms, as well as real life activities, where I wouldn't be tempted to show my love in this manner.

Sharing My Gifts

This has always been hard for me. Instinctively, demonstrating what I'm good at always felt like bragging. Maybe it's because I'm a middle child, but being modest is more comfortable for me. For example, my first few years of CrossFit I did less than I could. Other strengths lay hidden too. I didn't sing in front of others. No one really knows I'm a visual artist. I don't even display myself in makeup. I decided one of my values is to display my uniqueness, creativity, sense of humor, and wisdom. But *posting* these things online made the focus about people thinking highly of me. My focus now is to share without searching for that approval. I want to be free to share in the virtual world, too, but without the negative repercussions of validating my talents with likes.

Putting Myself First

Doing what I need to do for me is—shocker!—difficult. But it can be done. Putting myself first before my husband, my kids, my family, and my friends is hard but mandatory. This was an easy one to apply to social media. Even though it feels wrong to post content but not follow people on a newsfeed, I knew it was the formula I needed, the right way to create a good relationship with social media. It was also time to let me guide my own path.

Letting Others Help

Our family business does need to have a virtual presence. In addition, if I want to truly share my words, I also need somewhat of an online presence. This work can be done by me, or I can hire someone for social media if the resources allow. In addition, I can allow myself to not feel bad when I leave my children for an afternoon. I can ask others for help and trust that they want to. I can look to find value online if it allows me to share and collaborate with others (blogging, texting, etc.). Once I established my values, identifying how they fit in (or kept out) the virtual world was easy.

PROTECT SIMPLICITY:

- ***Extend your learning by reading about positive virtues***. I personally like the discussion of virtues from these books: *Atomic Habits, The 5 AM Club, and The Art of Living*. I learned examples of good virtues: being intrigued/open, genuine, tuned in, empathetic. I also saw the importance of practicing virtues: reciprocal warmth, uniqueness that is practical, information-seeking, lifelong learning, prudence, seeking perspective, and staying curious.

- ***Journal and reflect:*** *Are you living out your values?* This exercise can help to find where various technologies are helping or hurting and then lead you to make necessary changes. It might help you see that you may be living out these values already in the real world and need far less online time than you thought you did.

- ***When possible, hire a social media content creator.*** Budget for someone to create content for advertising purposes. We have done this for our small business, and I plan to do so if any marketing is needed for my future endeavors.

- ***Spread joy the old-fashioned way.*** I advocate for a return to vintage ways of showing love that often seem forgotten, like sending cards and letters. My artist neighbor reignited my creative spirit when she taught me to use magazines, junk mail, and old greeting cards to craft personalized cards. It's a therapeutic activity that not only fosters creativity but also strengthens connections with loved ones. Adding personal touches and mailing these creations can be complemented by listening to classical music to further awaken artistic instincts. These methods make us feel more connected, contrasting with social media posts that sometimes do the opposite.

- ***Share photos digitally with a small number of close friends and family.*** I've enjoyed sharing photos through digital frames. I'm also working on a private Instagram account for sharing photos with close family and friends.

- ***Engage in conversations with others who share your values in regard to technology.*** My husband and I have built a fitness community that keeps us accountable to being healthy and fit. Daily attendance with a group of others with similar health goals makes it easy. Just like with fitness, if I want to strengthen my mission to utilize technology intentionally, I need to spend time with others who share it.

My hope is that within our friend groups we can unite in our decisions. Therefore, making big decisions, such as delaying the purchase of smartphones for our kids, feels less radical and more normal.

- ***Make life so good you forget about the screen.*** Sure, there are ways the screen can enhance my values. But I look to mostly live them out in the real world. With any time that is left, I can carry over those values into the virtual world. You can do this by living out your strengths. I took a survey that a therapist recommended called the VIA character strength survey. The idea is that you find out what your top five strengths are, and in living them out, you experience greater life satisfaction.

Chapter 4

Unfollow Relationship Saboteurs

The main thing is to keep the main thing the main thing.

—Stephen Covey

Since I have been highlighting many negatives about social media and smartphones, let me offer some positive features. Compared to corded phones limiting location usage, long distance charges within the States, and offering no screen for instant communication, smartphones offer a pretty limitless ability to connect. We now socialize with far more people, across vast locations. And we can see into the lives of others via social media. Once, we had no access to know what an acquaintance ordered at an anniversary dinner, or what they wore! Now we can view every detail down to the music they chose to pair with the memory. We make and maintain connections that couldn't have happened otherwise.

But as is my theme, I will touch on the flip side of the coin. This ease of communication is a double-edged sword. Today's avenues for communicating and socializing put the quality of our main relationships at risk. At least they did for me. The digital age turned my social life into a tornado of overwhelm. I found my introverted self spinning from the various pulls for attention from online "friends" (like me! respond to me!), our loved ones in person, and loved ones online. (Because you're not a good friend unless you 1) know what they've been up to, and 2) give them likes or virtual shout-outs.) I was left with a social problem: I had too many relationships to manage and too many expectations for maintaining them. Social media and text messaging, which was supposed to make our relationships stronger, did the opposite. I began examining what was making my relationships suffer so I could make better decisions in the future.

First, attention given to online friends takes time I can't spare. Social media has its own set of criteria of what it means to be a friend. Hundreds, or even thousands, of virtual friends, requires a lot more relationship-management. Meanwhile, relationship maintenance outside the screen stayed the same. I had my true friends—people I know in real life and see or talk to with my voice. Then, depending on which platform, there were the many other relationships to manage, with their own set of criteria.

Being fully present on Facebook meant "first day of school" pics to like, groups to manage, and vacation photos to ooh and aah at. Instagram had the "like for a like" system—a composite of one-plus hours a day—making sure not to leave anyone out. It was paying careful attention to not like just some of my friends'/acquaintances'/frenemys' posts. Because if you like one person's, others will see it, so it seemed vital to like everyone's posts in that circle. And there are a million circles. So it was basically just a lot of liking. There was also the pressure to post to my friends, or audience, which meant time-consuming preparation of photos and corresponding cute captions.

There is some research that there is a limit to how many relationships we can maintain. A concept called Dunbar's Number. It says that around 150 is the typical number of people we can keep track of and consider part of our ongoing social network. And with the new "need" to maintain social media friendships in addition to real ones, I'm pretty sure we are all performing above our friendship limitations. When I put too many eggs in my virtual basket, my real life friendships suffered. I was spending time interacting with people I didn't even know at the cost of time with my close friends and family.

I noticed something else that changed my relationships. Social media made me see some friends in a more negative light. This could arguably be a positive because social media acts as a filter in helping eliminate the "too many friendships" problem. However, sometimes it was a family member, so ideally someone I wanted to maintain a positive relationship with. Nonetheless, sometimes what I saw on the newsfeed complicated my feelings toward them. Some posts (divisive topics or the observation of a false persona) made me rethink how I felt about them. It made some of my relationships confusing, to say the least.

Another culprit was the fear of missing out and its influence to make me say yes to too many social events. Group text messages led to peer pressure. Social media led to seeing what events others were at, being invited to many more (think graduation parties of long-lost friends' kids), and advertisements of activities. I said yes every time I was invited to go out. I engaged in every group conversation. I signed my kids up for activities because everyone else in the group chat took the bait. Seeing what others were signing up for on social media encouraged me to sign up, which is what it's supposed to do. It changed how often I went out, how much I went on various social media platforms, and what I did for entertainment. The more text chains I was a part of the more I overextended myself.

Finally, the pressure, or at least the impulse, to make notifications go away made me prioritize what was on the screen over who I was in front of. Time is precious, and it's essential to be present with people in person instead of distracted by our phones. Dinner and bedtime are the only times I have to talk with my kids, so I hated anything that interrupted these moments. The pressure of the incessant texting and emails, and the pressure to respond, took away from my relationships in the flesh.

I wanted so badly to enjoy communicating this way—to be all-in on social media and messaging. I wanted it to enhance my relationships. But I kept thinking about what managing friendships was like pre-social media and smartphones: knocking on each other's door, hanging out, talking on the phone. It was simple. So I put my focus into getting some of those practices back in alignment with utilizing technology minimally. Like all topics of digital life, I went on a mission to use tech for all its worth and get rid of the excess. I looked to creating habits where I connected less in order to gain more out of my relationships.

PROTECT SIMPLICITY:

- ***Call or have a video chat with your friends.*** When my friend and her best friend couldn't find time to connect, they created a habit of calling each other on their way to work. I like to call others on long drives or when I take walks, or FaceTime family for a virtual coffee or glass of wine. These types of interactions don't allow the phone to be used for any other purpose. There is no temptation to scroll or multitask because the device is being held or propped. This practice helps maintain a personal touch in relationships.

- ***Do what you love, and the friends will follow.*** Prioritize in-person activities that help you make new friends and stay in touch with your current ones. My daily social needs are met with a 6:00 a.m. workout class, lunch with coworkers, occasional walk with a friend, and time with the family. As an introvert, any extra social commitments feel excessive. Purposefully scheduling these activities has reduced the need for additional social plans. My friend, who was also trying to become more intentional in her relationships, said to me, "I'm a friend of convenience." In realizing I was the same, I started guiding my social life around the idea to "do what I love, and the friends will follow." It made me feel less worried about saying no other invitations, or keeping up others online, because I was confident I was doing enough.

- ***Accept changes in social circles.*** Not being active on social media doesn't make you a bad friend or family member. My spouse helped me understand that maintaining relationships isn't solely my responsibility. It's okay if some people drift away; our values will naturally guide us to the right connections.

- ***Proactively communicate.*** Being online less can be isolating. Clear communication is important. Let loved ones know your goals related to screen-life balance. Share tech behaviors you struggle with and ask them to share any they have. Discuss specific ways you can meet in the middle to maintain the relationship. Sharing relatable content is fun. I encourage those I am close with to text me relatable reels and funny memes. I set a timer anytime I decide to look for ones to share as well. When I felt the impact from not sharing photos with family, I opened a private Instagram account for that purpose. Ask questions when you get together. It can feel awkward to enter a conversation not knowing what someone has been up to. If they regularly post online there is a certain expectation their friends follow along. People like to talk and share, so I use the power of active listening. I find asking them questions and letting them talk about their lives and interests is a win-win.

- ***Be choosy with text engagement.*** In recent years, I found myself in numerous group texts. At one point I was in four different "mom group" chats (all titled "book club," yet only one truly was). I found most did not fulfill their promise to be "my tribe." They didn't deliver on their promise of connection. I also found that having too many text message groups to manage regularly caused me to stop texting everyone regularly. I have learned to prioritize relationships that truly matter, focusing on those who are there for me in times of need. The right relationships can go the distance without incessant text messaging. I've also found text messaging can add to a relationship as long as it's done with limitations.

- ***Use social media in stealth mode***. My sisters and I like to say our brother uses Facebook in stealth mode. We'll be together and he'll reference something he saw on there. But we didn't know he was active on there because he doesn't like or comment on anything. As is my vibe, I try to find inspiration in what works for others. I like to hop on a friend's page who I'm going to see soon, delegate time to view their virtual photo album, and send them a text about it, or mention it when I see them. Or I'll check on a family member's page to keep up with the ages of my many nieces and nephews.

- ***Use non-social media apps to improve communication.*** Put close family and friend's important information under their contact in your phone. I used to check Facebook every day just so I could see whose birthday it was. To avoid heading to the vortex, I started recording addresses (for card sending and in-person visits), birthdays with ages, and names of children and spouses in my calendar and contact list. Use a digital calendar to schedule regular meet-ups. When we are busy socializing online, digital interactions can easily take the place of more meaningful, in-person ones. Actively scheduling time to meet in person is an effective way to combat this.

Chapter 5

Unfollow Leading by Bad Example

Children will be who you are, so be who you want them to be.

—David Bly

A few years back, I was assigned to assess the academic achievement skills of a little boy. He was a first grader struggling with off-task behavior for a couple of years. The background I was given revealed that he was very bright but didn't quite know how to do school yet. I was told the boy simply wanted to be loved, and technology overuse at home seemed to be an issue. They also told me he liked to read to his brother but needed more books. At night, his mom would give him an iPad to watch until he fell asleep. I assessed his reading comprehension by having him read stories and answer questions about what he read. He accurately answered them, demonstrating the skill of using both the text and outside knowledge. Sadly, his observation of outside life was more influential in answering one of the questions. The story is of a mother and child having a picnic. I asked him what the mother was doing at the park. His response was, "Well, the mom sits on the bench and looks at her phone, and the kid plays on the playground."

The beginning of the 2024–2025 school year staff meeting started with our principal asking us not to be hypocrites. It was our second year of disallowing smartphones in classrooms. She said, "Since we are raising our expectations for our school, teachers should not be using cell phones for personal reasons either. If we are raising our expectations for students, we need to hold the same standards for ourselves." It was the reminder I needed to stop walking down the hall, multitasking on my smartphone, nearly bumping into students while walking to class.

I was at a college hockey game where I observed this disengaged behavior from a middle-aged man. It was subtle but noticeable. My family and I were in row four, and the man in front of us in row three. The game was action-packed, and with such close seats you would have to work hard not to be engaged. But work hard this man did—on tending to his phone. He didn't look up from the screen for more than two minutes at a time, texting or surfing the entire game. My child and I pointed it out at the same time. I was proud to see that he thought it wrong for a little box to distract from the people and action around you. I used this as an example of how adults are not guaranteed to be someone you should model your behavior after.

Parents, who are their child's biggest influencers, seem to be modeling behaviors that may not always be ideal. I knew what I was doing wasn't working. But everywhere around me I saw parents and teachers and older individuals partaking in the same hypnotic behaviors without introspection. To generalize them as older and wiser may no longer be accurate. What would life have been like if my mom was an aspiring influencer? My childhood certainly had the formula to be a viral YouTube channel. As a middle child of seven, our home was surrounded by clutter, chaos, and laughter. Before *The Real World* introduced the concept of reality TV, we'd often joke, "What if our lives were videotaped? People would crack up!"

If my mom had chosen to showcase (rather, *exploit*) our upbringing, how different would my childhood have been? Would she have us going through outtakes until the perfect scene was acted out? As a child, family photos were enough of a stressor, let alone Christmas concerts and Easter Mass in a dress. What if she forced us into little outfits and interrupted our play to make us strike a pose? What if she choreographed our dances and we never got to make up our own? Would my parents have been glued to their phones? How would my life be different today if they were obsessed with YouTube viewer stats, and their mood was reliant on how well received a video was? This is eerily dystopian and, sadly, the reality of many children today. It makes me wonder what the repercussions are on those whose parents are living this way. We are only on verge of finding that out.

When the digital age came into full swing in the early 2000s, I caught myself revolving my life around it. I got out of the trance before any major damage was done. Living behind a screen wasn't how I wanted to live my life, and it's certainly not the fate I want for my children. This life of no relaxing, no being in the moment, always doing, doing, doing and never feeling good enough is not fulfilling. I want to positively influence the young people around me I am lucky enough to be around. I want younger generations to have a much easier time learning to coexist in a healthy way with a digital world. I know the first step in making it right for them is to make it right for me.

PROTECT SIMPLICITY:

- ***Spread your influence in "real life" communities.*** There are a lot of great online communities. However, my overall pursuit has been to fill up on time outside the screen, to make life so great I mostly forget about the screen. In this pursuit, I've found that I can influence outside of social media. I like to do so by engaging in a variety of communities (fitness, church, school, apparel, art, blogging, etc.). By diversifying your involvement, you can learn a lot, meet a diverse group of people, and positively impact them in person.

- ***Model enjoyment of non-digital activities.*** Encouraging children to engage in non-tech activities like puzzles, bracelet-making, or simply breathing exercises can be challenging if you're not leading by example. Experiment with doing non-digital activities in front of them that provide a more sustainable dopamine boost. If I start building a Lego city, there's a high chance my children will join me. If we're not careful to model non-digital ways to relax, ease boredom, and be entertained, the screen may be the only thing young people know to turn to. Sitting together as everyone engages in calming activities of their choice, like reading alongside the kids as they play, can be very effective.

- ***Verbalize your use of technology as a tool.*** Demonstrate a separation between work and leisure by verbalizing your use of technology. Talk to your kids about the apps you allow on your phone and why. When I am using my smartphone, I make it a point to say aloud which tool I'm using. For instance, say, "I am writing my book right now," or "I am using this as a camera right now." This practice helps children see the ways technology can be used beyond craving dopamine and validation. Where screens are part of the job, I try to demonstrate this openly. If using technology for a side hustle or work, using a laptop to signify the difference. As a small business owner, my spouse uses a scheduler app for posting on the business page and for sending weekly newsletters. I occasionally write on paper instead of using a computer to show my young kids, who are just now learning how to write, that I still value the skill of writing. Find ways to let your kids engage with you on technology you find useful. Displaying a digital calendar and task list they can use lets them experience a productive way of engaging with technology.

- ***Avoid referencing what's trending on social media (and scrolling on social media) in front of young people.*** Kids watch and observe us more than we know. Like the student who observed that moms sit on benches, scrolling on their phones, they are learning that what people are posting online is important. If they see enough adults gazing at phones and discussing viral videos, I fear they will stop short of striving toward any other hobbies. Worse, they will strive for nothing more than to be viral online themselves. I don't want to do anything that contradicts the emphasis that what we do in life does not need to be validated online. The habit of seeking validation online is difficult to break, and I certainly didn't want it for my kids.

- ***Share personal tech struggles.*** We've had to navigate new digital landscapes without prior role models. I have the opportunity to provide young people around me with strategies, skills, and anecdotes to help them manage their digital experiences. This includes dealing with my social media disappointments or peer pressure related to smartphone ownership. I like to talk to them about how the smartphone can pull me away from more important things. I share how I feel bad about myself when I spend time on social media apps. How I feel bad when I allow them too much time on a screen. I find it helpful to reference celebrities they may know who face similar struggles. Those who similarly have their children wait to have one-to-one screens (Joanna Gaines and Steve Jobs, to name a few). I think it's important to discuss mistakes I've made with technology and share my efforts to improve. This awareness and honesty gives me a fighting chance at navigating the digital age with awareness and balance.

- ***Show and tell all the things a smartphone includes.*** I don't want to assume my kids know all the features of a smartphone. I also don't want them to find out from any of their friends who own one. Showing them the various features, good and bad, might help them make better decisions when they have their own. This is especially helpful when we get into discussing why they are not getting their own smartphone until a certain age.

- ***Have a home for smartphones.*** We leave our smartphones in a designated spot when home. I like to leave the sound on for phone calls to mimic the old days when phones were mounted on the wall. We model by example. When our kids' friends come over with a smartphone, we show them where we put ours (on a flat charger on top of the mantle) and say that we expect them to do the same while visiting. We let them know they are welcome to check it when they need to. This prevents their time together being reduced to sitting on the couch, scrolling through TikTok or YouTube. This even applies to when I am driving them around in the car. In giving a young friend a ride home one day, I saw how my son was clueless on how to "entertain" his friend, who spent the downtime looking down at his phone. At such an early age, children are already losing the ability to engage in small talk with each other when they have the phone as a crutch. So I politely asked him for the phone and put it on my dashboard for the rest of the ride.

Chapter 6

Unfollow Refusing to Embrace Discomfort

We're terrified of being bored.

—Nicholas Kardaras

I failed my first driving test. I've never told anyone that. Not my spouse, my sisters, or my friends. I'd characterize it as one of my most embarrassing moments. But I admit it now because my dad making me go back to school after that morning of failure is a life lesson I use as a parent today. My parents had standards that they kept to. One was attending school. (I thought this was everyone's standard until I became an educator, but it is definitely not.) My driver's test was in the morning. I parallel parked perfectly but couldn't make a left-hand turn to save my life. Thankfully, I didn't end my life or the instructor's that day. I begged my dad to take me home so I could sulk. He took me back to school instead. It was a day of discomfort, but I was pushed to carry on, and in doing so I learned I could work through tough moments.

The completion of a Tough Mudder event convinced me of the power of embracing discomfort in my adult life. One of the obstacles required little five-foot me to dangle from a man's legs on a near-vertical wall as several teammates used me as a rope. The obstacle was complete with the pulling up of our remaining teammates: two adults, twice my size, up the wall. Instead of leaving me gasping, the obstacle left me high. I know it's because of my commitment to doing daily workouts. Waking up to attend a 6:00 a.m. class Monday through Friday is difficult each and every morning. It's in the practice of working through regular bouts of discomfort that I am able to muster through larger ones.

Going back to my youth, I think about how my parents rarely bailed my six siblings and me out when we experienced discomfort. We didn't have a say on what entertainment there was in the car. I can still hear the sound of the AM radio static my siblings and I had to endure when we drove with my dad (not to mention his driving and cigarette smoking). We wore what we were told. As a tomboy, wearing a parochial school uniform with a skirt every day felt like torture. We had to trust that our ride would come for us. At least once a month I got to experience the discomfort of not knowing whether my parents were running late from picking me up from soccer practice, or if they had forgotten entirely. We were expected to do hard things. My paper route job required me to get up at 6:00 a.m. on weekends and was definitely character-building. I know now that these experiences served a purpose for what I can get through today.

Working through tiny discomforts build up tolerance for greater discomforts. I fear that in today's digital world, with its quick fixes, it's too easy to rid ourselves of small but important discomforts. I'm working harder than ever to push through the temptation to do so and embrace discomfort as it comes. Every time I do, it feels like I've cracked some code. I read an article that had an interview with an Olympic runner. The runner explained how athletes, despite years of training, never get to a point where the task is easy. Instead, they just get good at accepting pain throughout the moment. This mindset is well-known in the CrossFit world. You put in the work, you watch yourself get stronger, you feel yourself get faster, but every workout remains a challenge. Applying the mentality of accepting pain helps me tune into the physicality of the workout and do more than I ever thought I could.

Fear is a discomfort that can cause us to avoid things entirely. The first time I ever sang on stage got me hooked. But I wouldn't have even stepped foot on the stage in the first place if I let the fear to do so guide me. Fifteen years later, and I am still in a state of discomfort every time I step on stage. It doesn't matter if it's a big show or karaoke at a bar; I experience fear. By acknowledging it and moving forward anyway, I am able to experience the high that comes with creating that type of energy with an audience. If I let that fear stop me, I'd be limiting the experiences that come with sharing the joy I intend to spread.

One of the biggest hurdles of discomfort I work through is the feeling of boredom. I think it is a major struggle for most. When I realized some of my worst habits arose from that discomfort, I was able to start knocking them. In the evenings, when my responsibilities were done for the day, a freight train of discomfort used to roll in. It should have been a time of relief. The lunches were made, the kitchen was clean, and the kids were settled in front of the television. Instead, a bad feeling of uselessness kicked in. A miniature sense of empty-nest syndrome guided me to pour a glass of wine, eat some snacks, and scroll on my phone night after night after night. When I decided I no longer wanted this routine, I found I couldn't easily drop it. I had to practice being present with the knowledge that boredom is uncomfortable. In acknowledging that it is there, I was allowing myself to be separate from it.

Having children provides new challenges. Throw in a digital world and it's a whole new ballgame. I want to model the way my parents taught me when encountering uncertainty. However, when fear, boredom, and anxiety arise in those I have the honor of raising, or when their behavior results in me feeling anger, it is hard not to go for quick fixes. Quick fixes that weren't available to my parents. The habitual use of quick fixes to work out life's discomforts can only make getting through tougher moments harder. Whatever we do grows stronger. In using the screen for a quick fix with my children's discomforts too often, I noticed a harmful pattern forming. They went for the screen each and every time a discomfort arose. They used it to avoid as well as to bypass moments. Then, in times that I held strong and disallowed the screen/pacifier, we ran into more trouble. When it was removed as an option, they had little practice, or even knowledge, of other means for working through tough moments.

I worry that children today lack the opportunity to work through tough moments. I'm grateful that I didn't have the crutch of the screen. I would have chosen staring at one over fighting with my siblings, counting cars on car rides, and writing in my journal each and every time. I know that I wouldn't have the grit I have today if I did. Young people today can potentially pacify all their discomforts away. If instead of accepting and working through small discomforts (boredom in the car or waiting room, the anxiety of responsibilities, fights with siblings), then how will they be prepared to work through greater challenges when they arise?

As I complete almost two decades as an educator, I can't help but notice the impact an intolerance of discomfort has on students. When cell phones were allowed in classrooms (a practice that ended in our 2023–2024 school year), I observed students glued to their phones during both structured and unstructured times. In those years of allowance, they rarely had to work through even the discomfort of small talk with their peers during lunch or lulls in class time. Many of them went entire school days (and some entire days) with their attention directed on their screen.

Many educators will tell you there is an increasing lack of grit in kids today. When faced with challenges, they will cower under pressure. I see it at both the elementary and the high school level. There seems to be an increasing lack of motivation, drive, and ability to problem-solve. Parents bail their kids out at any mention of ill-feelings and remove any obstacle at the first sign of distress in their children (thus forcing educators to do so as well). Teachers are forced to lower their standards to appease overbearing parents (who mainly have good intentions). Students are excused from work, and often out of daily attendance, at any utterance of negative emotion. Many of these emotions are useful if accepted and guided to work through. I observe an unwillingness for parents to push their children to do hard things. Even if a child desires to work through their own problem, it is often already worked out by their parent. High schoolers don't have to discuss any conflict with a teacher themselves because their parents intervene by emailing on their behalf. Parents of elementary-aged children text each other about minor arguments instead of letting them work it out themselves on the playground.

I think back to my own days as a student, where I'd dreadfully get ready, wishing I didn't have to go to school. If my parents allowed me to stay home when I had those bouts of what I now know was anxiety, I would have developed an inability to attend regularly like I see in so many students today. As parents, we want our children to develop good mental health. Research shows that there is a link between self-efficacy and an internal locus of control with better mental health.[1] Those who believe in their own ability to succeed in specific situations (self-efficacy) persevere through challenges. Those with a belief that they are in control of their own outcomes (internal locus of control) have greater resilience when they face challenges.[2] Studies suggest that those who possess a strong sense of self-efficacy and internal locus of control are more independent and resilient. In addition, they are more likely to experience higher levels of well-being and lower levels of anxiety and depression. In shielding young people from encountering and working through tough tasks we could be hindering their development of these important skills.

When discomfort arises, we want it to go away. We fight it with the first available fixer, or we avoid what might cause it. The digital age makes it easy to do so. But it seems we are cheating ourselves when we do. We are trading long-term growth for immediate comfort. In our avoidance of challenging situations, we are missing out on what could be amazing opportunities. It's in facing minor discomforts that we learn and grow. Committed to not following suit, I continued the practice of embracing discomfort.

PROTECT SIMPLICITY:

- ***Have an ongoing project for when boredom strikes.*** You better believe I stopped experiencing boredom when I gave myself a strict deadline for the first draft of this book. I saw the same thing when my kids began making iron bead projects. They were invested in finishing whatever they had started on them so when there were breaks in the day, it was their go-to project.

- ***Actively notice and sit with discomfort.*** Initially, I perceived discomfort as negative—whether emotional, physical, or general unease—and something to be eradicated. However, I learned that accepting pain is crucial because emotions serve a purpose. By acknowledging them, I find their purpose and respond thoughtfully rather than reacting impulsively. I calmly identify the emotion and acknowledge the physical sensations it brings. By accepting discomfort, I allow myself time to decide how to handle it, whether by sitting peacefully with it or finding an activity that aligns with my values. This practice helps develop patience and creativity.

- **Use mantras.** When temptations arise, having a prepared mantra is beneficial. My favorite is: "Sometimes life is boring and hard." I keep it visible on my refrigerator and share it with my children as needed. In challenging workout moments, thinking, "I am in a state of suffering right now" allows me to acknowledge and work through the discomfort.

- *Limit the use of the screen as a pacifier.* Allowing children to experience boredom cultivates patience and imagination, essential skills for development. According to Nicholas Kardaras in Glow Kids, reducing screen time during early developmental years encourages creativity and cognitive growth.[3] Unfortunately, tech pacifiers are readily available these days. But do you ever stop to think about how the same reason we wean young children off of baby pacifiers is why we should wean them off of tech ones? We want them to work to have independence in soothing themselves. Many kids go from school activities to structured activities to online activities, leaving little time for imaginative play. Be choosy with when the screen is given, versus automatically providing it for short car rides, waiting for food, etc. It's too early to know what overuse of digital pacifiers will do to their attention span, ability to practice patience, or willingness to tolerate waiting. Personally, I don't want to find out. Instead of automatically providing a screen, I am observing what my child needs in that moment. Are they bored? Hungry? Feeling unloved? Then, I find non-tech ways to solve that problem. My hope is that with practice, scaffolding, and time, they will come up with the screen alternatives themselves. When the use of tech as a pacifier is turned to as a needed escape for yourself or your kids, limiting its use in other parts of the day.

- ***Challenge yourself to spend longer periods without your phone.*** Not long ago, going hours without easy access to a phone was normal and not anxiety-inducing as it often is today. We have grown used to being able to contact others at any time, and our phones have become our all-in-one devices—even our main source of escape. Accidentally letting my phone die taught me the value of occasional disconnection. During a medical emergency with my son, I spent thirty phone-less hours in the ER. That experience became a form of exposure therapy, showing me there was nothing to fear in being without my phone. Though having it would have been comforting, I managed, and even appreciated the quiet. I adapted by finding new ways to communicate, write, entertain myself, and seek comfort. Start small: leave your phone in another room, then gradually try leaving it at home when you go for a walk or a night out. Incremental steps like these can help you build confidence in your ability to disconnect.

- ***Foster independence.*** It's our responsibility to guide children toward healthy activities and personal achievements even when they push back. Instead of rescuing my children from every challenge, I allow them to work through difficulties with my support. Guiding them to work through conflicts with their peers fosters autonomy and problem-solving skills. Teaching them how to use a phone to schedule playdates, or respond to messages pertaining to their plans, helps them gain confidence. We can increase the boundaries of where they can venture out without much technology. A watch that only tells the time can allow children to practice time management and responsibility when they are given a curfew.

- ***Use an app blocker for any apps left on your phone.*** There are many app blockers on the market, so experiment to find one that works for you. I turned to the use of one when I found myself hypnotically opening the same two apps dozens of times throughout the day. Now, when an impulse guides me to check the app, I see that it is blocked, and I lose interest or ambition to do the work it requires me to open it.

Chapter 7

Unfollow Your Bad Tech Habits

You do not rise to the level of your goals. You fall to the level of your systems.

—James Clear

I came home from the gym one Monday morning to find the house quiet. At my usual 7:15 a.m. arrival, this was abnormal as I expected my oldest child to be watching television in the living room. The silence was a telltale sign that he was downstairs on the Xbox. Our family rule then was an 8:00 a.m. start time on weekends only (and only with our permission). I went to awaken the other boys but noticed that all of them were missing. They had all taken advantage of our increasingly loosening rules regarding video games.

Our boys know that we secretly like them on the game at times so we can get stuff done, and if we leave the controllers out and they hop on the game at will, we will only sometimes take them away. They also know that if they bug us enough, we will almost always give in. Finally, they have the belief that since it is summer, all rules go out the window. Unfortunately, their belief has not been entirely false.

That same summer morning, my 7:30 a.m. alarm notified me it was time to make the kids' snacks. I had purposely signed them up for short bursts of summer activities that started in the morning. Getting out of the house and doing something purposeful always leads to a much smoother day. Unfortunately, it also means I don't get a break from the morning rush during the summer break. This weird mix of summer lax on the screen usage rules with the need to get out of the house on time caused extra conflict. When they'd sneak down to play video games, I'd get extra jobs. Not only did I prepare their breakfast, but I had to scream down at them to come up to eat it. I prepared every single thing they needed for the day, then screamed warning after warning through the floor to pry them off the game. As I yelled for them to come upstairs for the tenth time, while getting myself ready along with all their things, I asked myself, *How did we get here?*

It dawned on me that I had been creating and solidifying a habit where they got to relax while I worked extra hard. It didn't make me feel good to scream at them, and it didn't start any of our days off right. Although I expressed anger at them, I was really mad at myself for engaging in a game of take away and give in: taking the video games away, threatening to get rid of them, then promptly giving them back when I got sick of saying no.

Getting right to work in the morning on lunches, snacks, and outfits for the boys was hard for me too. Sure, to a certain extent it is my role as their parent to help prepare them for their day. But it is also my role to teach them independence and cooperation. I realized I had created a habit that disallowed them to do any of the morning work. I, too, would love to simply awake and make my way to the television. I would also love to stay seated and call for my cereal to be brought in. I would love to never be responsible for putting my dirty dishes in the sink. In doing all these things for them, I was strengthening the habit for it to happen again and again. They would not grow out of it when they were older, and certainly not when they became teenagers.

I was mad that we were caught in that cycle, and not just in the mornings. They were decreasing in their ability to be the slightest bit bored. I was decreasing in my ability to tolerate their whining and fighting, causing me to give in too often. How my husband and I waived on our allowance of screen use depended on our mood or on how much we needed to get done that day. I was furious with myself for strengthening their habit of easing boredom with a screen. The result seemed to be an inability to find other means of comfort, making any time without the screen unbearable for the entire family.

I knew that getting angry at myself or at them wouldn't fix the issue. I had to think about it rationally. I realized the cycle could most likely be solved by changing our habits. We developed some bad habits, and I was inadvertently making them too easy to keep. We are influenced by what's in front of us. We want the easiest route to pleasure or the avoidance of pain, so whatever I was allowing to be in front of us was a major culprit. After years of avoiding working out in the morning, I found that one simple act made me do it consistently. Laying out my clothes in the morning was the key for me. Knowing I had already done that small step told my early morning brain it was okay to get up. I wasn't going to make it think too hard.

My kids will not simply make the decision to prepare lunches on their own. They will not just do it on command out of the blue. Just like I set up a scaffold for myself to work out in the morning, they need support to get started on tasks I'd like them to complete as well. And it may take time.

We can't will our way out of bad habits. If something I'm working to avoid is in my face, I will not avoid it. When smartphones were allowed at our high school, students were never going to will themselves away from their screens. We had to create that physical boundary for them. Quite frankly, it was our responsibility to do so. We buy our kids extra toys thinking enough of them will keep them away from the screen. We can try to lure with balls and bats, STEM inventions, crafts, and Legos all we want, but if the screen is an option, those toys will go unused. They will sit and collect dust in their unused playrooms.

When it comes to bad tech habits specifically, using screens to pacify is the habit I wanted to eliminate the most. I used them as babysitters many times before realizing what I was doing. I ultimately gave the controllers back each time because I was stuck in a bad habit of easing their boredom, and my annoyance of their boredom, with something that worked every time. I increased video game time, or threw them my smartphone, so I could "get things done" or talk to my friends. I felt validated because *everyone else was doing it.* Repeatedly bailing them out with a screen eliminates any need for them to figure out boredom for themselves. They lose experiences, time to develop their imagination, and the ability to cope when a screen is not present. And that is not fun for anyone. It was time to look back to simpler times for inspiration. Why, when television programming was a thing, were not many good shows on during the day? It's because they knew people were off living during that time. Back then, living guided the screen. It was living first, then came the screen with whatever time was left in the day. Today, the screen is available anytime we want.

PROTECT SIMPLICITY:

- ***Commit to the identity you want to have***. I have a running tally of areas in my life I want to improve upon. The habit of drinking alcohol was a big area for me. I tried many things. Finally, the combination of a friend potentially being diagnosed with cancer and me having to schedule a follow-up mammogram finally got me to decide that if I ever got diagnosed with cancer, I didn't want to feel like I possibly caused it because I couldn't muster through an evening without a cheap glass of wine. From that day on, I took on the identity that I am someone who puts healthy things in my body, and it stuck. I dropped the daily glass of wine and significantly reduced how much I drank socially. *"Our family does not play video games at will"* was my next identity to take on. This meant that for a while, I had to hide the video game controllers from myself to limit how much I gave in. I also had to stop bringing my smartphone to places where my youngest begged to have it.

- ***Put a cue on your smartphone.*** I ask myself, *Is this the best usage of my mental energy right now?* each time I reach for my phone. I think to myself, Is there a different tool I could use for this task? You can remind yourself to ask these questions with a physical cue on your smartphone, such as a rubber band or sticky note attached to your phone.

- *Have scaffolds ready.* Before I go to bed on school nights, I make sure the lunch containers are clean, and ready on the counter. Set up scaffolds to help your kids choose non-tech activities when boredom strikes. Providing clear and accessible options for activities can help ease boredom until imagination takes over. Having items ready to help them get started on chores and routines they can do will help set them up for eventual success with those as well. For myself, to avoid scrolling, I leave a book, journal and pen in the areas I tend to relax in. To avoid the habit of giving my phone to an impatient child at an appointment, I plan ahead by writing navigation instructions down if needed, so I can leave my phone at home.

- *Practice consistency and structure.* Four is the average number of times I hid the Xbox controllers each week on summer break. It is also the number of times I gave in and gave them back. Before summer began, I had plans of a daily structure, but every time the morning rush ended, I rationalized that they worked hard enough to get on the screen. The plans I had at arranging wiffleball games at the park, or bike rides, or hikes went to the wayside. I thought about how many other parents out there weren't planning those things either because their kids were already "entertained." Why change that setup? I knew I couldn't simply take those devices away for good. I had to have a structure in place. My spouse and I store our smartphones in what we call their "home." Doing this for other tech helps show that there is a time and place for their use. This also helps in hiding cues that will make it harder to start the things I know I will have a hard time stopping. Establish set procedures to avoid impulsively getting back into bad habits. Have structured procedures in place to prevent impulsive reactions to ease discomfort. For instance, use parental controls to limit time on video games. This way they can learn to practice their own allocation of time allowance on them. After only a few days of no Xbox days, the kids, even with friends over, evolved and stopped asking to play. They found other means of entertainment and fun. I was proud of us!

- ***Remove tech as an option***. The fighting during video gaming grew worse than their whining over wanting to play it, and actually trumped my giving in to it. When I stopped giving in, they fought me instead of each other. Anna Lembke, author of Dopamine Nation, says that having the anticipation and then failing to deliver something makes our pain reactors go into overdrive more than they would've had they not anticipated it.[1] In leaving the Xbox controllers out as a viable option, or having my phone sitting on my lap at every occasion, I am conditioning them to believe those are options. We now proactively negotiate when tech use is appropriate and remove it as an option for other occasions. We may allow video games for one leg of a trip, or a couple movies for a sick day, then remove the option. We bring out playing cards, paper, markers, and toys. Without the allowance of using a screen at their leisure, we can also strive on getting to the point where they are bored enough to practice daily living skills, such as chores or tasks needed to get themselves ready for the day.

- ***Leave non-tech activities in common areas of the house.*** If the worst part of disallowing video games for a while is a Nerf gun fight through my kitchen, I will take it. I like to leave board games, paper and markers, and Play-Doh on the kitchen table. I'll leave beach balls or an indoor basketball hoop and ball in the living room. Everyone knows the kitchen is where people want to be. And anyone who has children older than one with cute playrooms or kid-friendly basements knows that the kids want to be wherever you are. I dislike clutter like the rest, but I succumb to making the common areas readily available for fun or mindful activities that are tech-free. To jumpstart new habits for myself I like to start with easy options. For example, to get back into the habit of reading, starting with short or less dense books.

- ***Leave out a list of activities or chores that the family can do.*** The accomplishment of a chore can provide a dopamine rush. Sometimes my kids just don't know what to do. Anything that can make it easier for them to pick something is what I'm looking to do. A list on the refrigerator that includes the list of tasks we're looking to accomplish, as well as anything they can do, can help them both see how much work it takes to keep a home and provides ideas when boredom strikes. It also helps to provide an answer to the question we often get on days off with the kids: "What are we doing today?" It is unreasonable to assume the role of entertainer to our kids. It is also against my values to rely on technology to entertain my kids.

Chapter 8

Unfollow Bad Influencers

You are the company you keep.

—Michael Port

Our eldest is in the double digits, so the time for making big decisions regarding technology is now. Even though my husband and I agree with how we will handle smart devices, I found myself tempted to change my values based on the fact that one of his peers now had a smartphone. Peer pressure is funny like that. It affects us adults as much as it does kids. Upon learning many of his friends had a smartphone, I thought to myself, *Maybe we should rethink our stance.*

I've been a victim of peer pressure by kids younger than age ten before. I signed my kids up for different activities that I wasn't quite sure about because I feared they would be left out. I feared they would be left out when the other kids talked of those activities on the playground at school. I projected my fears onto them. I wanted to do what everyone else was doing for fear they would be outcast. I had to knock myself out of this juvenile mentality before all my values, intuition, and common sense went out the window. I wondered why I was essentially taking advice, or allowing myself to be influenced, by sources I didn't seek out. I am a lover of learning, so I enjoy reading the latest research on topics of interest to me. So why was I willing to adopt the behaviors of others point-blank? I asked myself, "Have I ever sought out advice from these individuals before? Are they who I would normally run a decision by? Would I take mental health advice from them? Have I ever asked them what they thought about one of my purchases before I bought something?" The answer was always no. So why would I let their decision to buy a smartphone for their child be something worth overlooking my own research? I stopped using others' behaviors as a case for what I should do. I vowed to be intentional with what I make of the influence around us. In the virtual world, Instagram duped me into believing that someone skilled in the area of highlighting their best selves and interacting with strangers at all hours of the day is who I should be seeking advice from. That if I regularly scrolled through pithy and inspirational quotes, I would thrive.

One of the experiments I tried after unfollowing accounts on Instagram was to add only accounts that had specific advice I was looking for. At the time, I was seeking advice for dealing with a narcissist, and Instagram somehow figured out I was a parent. Before I knew it, scrolling through and screenshotting parenting advice was my new hobby. I maybe would have taken the bait, but Instagram's idea of parenting advice consists of influencers making staged videos. I found the popular reels off-putting. People in my demographic desperately seeking attention from others by doing silly dances or playing tricks on their kids. I also hated their attempts to be relatable. The desperation to gain viewers was obvious in the videos that showcased them as 10 percent imperfect and 90 percent beautiful. I wanted none of it. Even at the expense of not bonding with friends over funny, relatable content, I stopped scrolling through reels completely. This also meant taking a break from seeking advice on social media. Scrolling for advice online, I realized, was just feeding that pesky bad habit of easing boredom. I was not actually gaining anything positive from the one-sided interactions. Advertisements disguised as inspiration could not hold a candle to seeing someone I admire do something admirable. I took my head out of the gutter (aka smartphone) long enough to see I could actively find my own influencers outside the screen.

In his book *The Art of Living,* Edward Sri discusses the importance of having a community of others who are "running after the same ideals." He said, "All education is ultimately about imitation. We're imitating others in a way of life." Further, he says, "We learn most about virtues, therefore, not in a book but by spending time with others whom we want to imitate."[1] There was a lot to be learned by observing those I did not want to emulate. But it's also important to find those who are living life the way you want to live as well. I knew there were people maintaining a virtual presence the right way that I could learn from too. This erased any need I thought I had for online inspiration. When it came to the real world, I developed a clearer focus on who to allow peer pressure from.

Conversations with someone on the same values wavelength as my own brings me back to my senses. Like the friend who grabbed my attention when she told me her active child developed a love of reading. Avoidant to reading at first, she explained how dramatically reducing screen time did the trick. She explained how after pushing through two tough weeks, she saw his transformation. Her seven-year-old even developed an imaginary friend. I was impressed by her openness and lack of care about what others may think. I took note of the words she speaks to her child when he is upset about his friends getting phones. Our conversation of shared values confirmed how important who you surround yourself with truly is.

PROTECT SIMPLICITY:

- ***Stick to the research.*** It's essential to remain steadfast in your beliefs by conducting thorough research. This involves taking time to verify information and ensuring it aligns with your values and goals. By doing so, you can confidently support and practice what you advocate for and encourage your children to do the same. Research shows smartphones are addictive. When I think of the peer pressure I felt to give my child a smartphone, I had to get back to my sound reasoning. Reasoning that others whom I am tempted to mimic may never think of. I want to put off how long my kids are slaves to the habit of checking text notifications as long as possible. To imagine an entire lifetime of checking a screen for text messages alone saddens me greatly. This sadness trumps any fear I have that my child will miss out from missing out on text messages from other child children.

- ***Limit online sources for advice and inspiration.*** When seeking guidance online, I carefully select my sources. I primarily use AI and Reddit, avoiding platforms like Instagram, TikTok, or Facebook, where influencers often have underlying motives such as product promotion or seeking validation through likes and comments. This approach keeps me focused on my values and mission. For instance, I participate in SubReddits that align with my life goals and consult groups like Wait Until 8th on Facebook for support related to parenting decisions. I've realized that genuinely valuable advice or life hacks will reach me through trusted channels.

- ***Control your social environment.*** One of my guiding principles comes from Josh Fields Milburn of The Minimalists Podcast: "You can change the people around you but you can't change the people around you."[2] I choose to spend time with people who share my values, as I feel more at ease and fulfilled after interacting with them. I discuss my fears, mistakes, and temptations with these individuals, who provide support and understanding. By following their examples and ignoring behaviors from others that don't align with my values, I maintain a positive social environment for myself and my family.

- ***Change your phone to grayscale.*** Most apps are made up of bright colors and flashy images for a reason. They attract our attention. They are the novelty our brains are looking for. Turning your phone to grayscale mode makes the experience of using your smartphone pretty boring. It can help make you less interested in what's on the screen, thus keeping your attention on the right things in the real world.

- ***Find the right balance of seeking out life hacks.*** Many of my friends reference TikTok or Instagram for recipes or hacks. I will say that as someone who is not on TikTok, or who doesn't scroll through Instagram, I still learn about these hacks through word of mouth. Therefore, I know I am not completely out of the loop on fun things to be learned. I do learn on Reddit. It makes me think about how we don't need to feel we have to be on all of the platforms to be in the know.

- ***Include the kids in your projects.*** Involving children in creative projects, like writing a story or helping you paint a room, provides them with hands-on experience. Establishing spaces where they can contribute to family projects, such as a lemonade stand or treehouse construction, provides memories as well as life skills. Let them see, and be involved in meaningful projects that happen in the real world.

- ***Find ways for kids to join in on family activities you bring them too.*** Outings where children tag along can add the same value as a school field trip. Patiently step away from your own activity to answer questions or provide them with an activity you are doing. Instead of allowing them to view a tablet the entire time, take some time to walk around with them during a sibling's sporting event. When they have to tag along to your workout, give them a mini workout to do. Share with them pieces of what you are doing and make it a game they have to do before they are allowed screen time. This allows them to get something out of the outing instead of simply the viewing of the same content they are constantly viewing.

Chapter 9

Unfollow Impressing the Online World Instead of Loved Ones in the Real One

Attempting to be an influencer is like being part of a corporation. You're sitting in the board room "hoping to impress the people I'm supposed to impress."
—*Joshua Fields Milburn, Everything That Remains*

Back in the day, I decided to put my creative energy toward a health-focused Instagram account to complement our fitness business. We didn't necessarily need it; business was doing fine. But it seemed like what entrepreneurs were *supposed* to do who had a skill to share. My skill being maintaining fitness while raising a family. There wasn't space in my life to add the job of virtual life manager. I also didn't want my family to see me on my phone constantly. But I jumped in at full force anyway.

The corner of the kitchen is where I did my dirty work. My hideout was the space between the sink and refrigerator. It was genius because I could throw my phone at a moment's notice. If I heard footsteps, I'd toss it and pretend to be tending to kitchen duties. The many tasks that came with the job drew me to that corner dozens of times a day. I thought I had the balancing act under control until I found myself increasingly short with others. When questioned, I adamantly blamed my irritability on the overwhelm of raising three boys under age five. I wasn't ready to admit it, but the task of maintaining this Instagram account was the culprit. Admitting that influencing others made me the worst influencer to those who mattered to me the most was powerful. Caring little about the progress I had made on the page, or the followers who may be expecting a post, I just stopped. Stepping away from the haze of the glowing screen helped me see the light. But it was a different kind of light. It was the light in my child's eye when I talked to him without simultaneously looking down at my phone.

I thought about all the ways we choose the screen over our loved ones. How we put so much effort into impressing others. When we post a family photo with the caption, "My life, my everything," do we also look our kids in the eye and speak those words aloud to them? When we post about our kids' miniscule or grand achievements, do we also congratulate them in person? Or have we become so focused on the virtual stage that we forget?

It's common today to celebrate people we love online. It's a positive thing about social media, right? Or is it? Did the quantity of people who posted "Happy Birthday" to you on Facebook make or break your day? How many times did you only say "Happy Birthday" or "Happy Anniversary" online? How many times did you say words to someone online that aren't entirely true? Why have we grown more comfortable telling our loved ones that we love them online instead of in person? Why do we now say meaningful things in front of a virtual audience instead of to someone's face? Are we too lazy, overworked, or busy, to look each other in the eyes anymore? Do we just like posting that much? It was only when I stepped back from the platforms I realized how mistaken my priorities had become. Left with the short end of the stick were my sons, real-life friends, husband, and even myself. So I made some changes to assure I am impressing those who matter most.

PROTECT SIMPLICITY:

- ***Impress your children with uninterrupted time.*** It's not realistic to be 100 percent focused on your kids. We work, have hobbies, and need at least a little space to keep sane. But small bouts of uninterrupted time are all it takes to impress my boys. Smiling along with them and engaging in their silly games bonds us like nothing else. Posting photos of the cool things they were doing only took me away from that in-the-moment parenting they need so much. Posting photos had zero positive affect on them personally as they don't check social media newsfeeds (thank goodness!). So snapping and sharing photos of them will never again be at the cost of this vital in-the-moment time.

- ***Engage in family activities.*** I schedule fewer activities for my kids these days and decrease their time on devices because overuse was causing too much conflict and distance. Our kids don't have their own tablets, and use of our smartphones is limited. We have one television for programs and one for video games. We enjoy watching shows together at the end of the day. The fighting they do as siblings is pretty average, unless video games are involved. When we reset the rules on video games use, we made it a family activity for a while. They felt loved to have us join in, so we were able to use that momentum and switch our habit to more family friendly activities like wiffleball, card games, and bike rides.

- ***Focus on showing affection in person.*** I think it's important to say that this is a no-judgement zone. Social media provides a virtual platform for spreading love and joy. I applaud those who post and like and sincerely enjoy that kind of engagement. I also recognize there are people who feel less lonely when they interact online, particularly on special days. Words that I posted online are words that come out as completely sarcastic when I say them aloud to my spouse. "Happy Anniversary to my better half! I am a better person because you are in my life." These things are true, but posting them online is not true to our relationship. I don't need him to post on our special days to feel loved, and he doesn't need me to either. Posting words about others in person is all the more powerful: "You are special for these reasons . . ." (classic birthday post), or "You're my best friend because . . ." (bestie humble brag post). Keeping them just between my loved ones and me feels more special.

- ***Do things just for the sake of doing them.*** Sometimes I felt like I did things just so I could post them online. I would dress my kids up in outfits for any day trip to get that impressive shot. Without the pressure to post, I enjoy what I'm doing without worrying about stopping to catch it for others to see. I worry less about snapping the perfect photo and in return I end up with amazingly candid shots. There's a freedom in this age to do things without anyone knowing you are doing them.

- ***Share photos you take of your kids with them.*** Upon taking a family photo, a six-year-old family member asked who I was posting it to, and I couldn't believe he knew the word "post." And not just the word "post" but the context. He wanted to know "who are you showing that to" so that he could determine if he should be worried about who is seeing it. This prompted me to assure I am letting my children know who is seeing their photos. To ensure my children get to enjoy the photos I take, I use several methods, such as sending them to a digital frame or creating photo books for them.

- ***Put your efforts into self-improvement.*** I took a step back when I found myself pretending to be someone else to influence others. By focusing on improving myself, I gained more clarity and made greater progress.

- ***Train your loved ones to say, "Stop looking at your phone."*** I used to hate when my spouse cued me to stop looking at my phone. I now embrace it and encourage my kids to do it too. It reminds me to put my phone back in its home and to get back to being present with them.

Chapter 10

Unfollow Adding Before Subtracting

Doing is never enough if you neglect being.

—Eckhart Tolle

As I walked my youngest to speech therapy one afternoon, we were behind a father and daughter who entered through the other door that read "Mental Health Services." The girl looked to be about twelve years old. In her hand was a smartphone. Based on my experience with high school students, I had an inkling for why she needed those services. I wanted to scream out an idea that might save both her and her father some time and energy: *It's the phone! Get rid of the phone!*

Students often share their difficulties regarding social situations. Although they don't overtly acknowledge a correlation between their problem and their phone or social media use, their descriptions suggest one. I gently advise them of various behaviors they have control over: blocking, deleting, and phone breaks. However, they seem to have an inability, if not unwillingness, to believe that using a device less could be a solution. It is an option that perhaps they can't fathom. Even in a conversation about it, they demonstrate an unwillingness to turn their attention away from the text chat, or newsfeed, that is reportedly wreaking havoc on their mental health—often engaging in the very thing as they complain to me about it.

I have noticed that we seem to be far more willing to *add* things to fix our problems than we are to *remove anything.* My siblings and I used to watch a show called *Tales from the Crypt.* It was probably too scary for us because I would never watch it now. For reference, *Goosebumps* is a watered-down version. Though I'd watched dozens of episodes, only one still haunts me. A couple had a curse that forced them to dance whenever a music box played. At the end of the episode, the music box never stopped, and they danced to their death. *Exhausted to death* is something I could unfortunately relate to.

Somewhere between college graduation and my second serious breakup, I went in search of a fix for my mood. The psychiatrist, as I had hoped, gifted me a generalized anxiety disorder diagnosis and a prescription. But as I left the appointment, my twenty-something self had a breakthrough: I should try removing a drug that could be causing my anxiety (caffeine) before adding one to fix it. It wasn't easy, but I switched to decaf. It worked. My anxiety eased up, and I never needed the prescription. After a two-week reset, my body was okay to enjoy coffee (in moderation) again. I found myself applying this tactic again once the digital age reared its ugly head.

As a fortieth birthday gift to myself, I sought out a therapist I had visited more than ten years prior when anxiety-depression 2.0 arrived. I began the appointment by saying even though I had performed as a singer for fifteen years, I had developed apathy for the craft. I explained how upcoming shows had always brought on many emotions: stage fright, anxiety with new songs, joy while practicing, and empathy and exhilaration as I sang the lyrics of great artists on stage. What brought me to her on this day was that during my recent performances, I had experienced a robotic, mild dread. I explained how I felt waves of anger, sadness, and brain fog that left me in a bad mood. With her help, I was able to define it. She said, "You've become so overwhelmed and overstimulated that you've become numb."

I picture my life as a playground seesaw. When good, it is evenly balanced with family time in a warm home, an interesting job, and fulfilling hobbies. When not so good, one end is piled with a lengthy to-do list and images of all my roles: wife, mother, scheduler, career-holder, shopper, organizer, friend, sibling, daughter, aunt, cleaner, family photographer, and social media sharer. My feet dangle, propped up on one end, unable to do anything.

Stuck. Immobile. *Numb.*

I got caught in the culture of more doing and less being. It encourages us to be efficient multitaskers. We're not encouraged to slow down or remove anything, but to instead ingest anything that will help us do even more, faster. A doing culture with the addition of technology made me focus so much on getting tasks done, I was hardly living through the doing of any of them, let alone moments that mattered.

If not for myself, I needed to take something, *anything* off my plate, if only for the sake of modeling to my kids what calm, non-stressed adulthood looks like. Doing more tasks seemed to equate with being a good parent. Not only doing more to maintain a household and family calendar, but also giving our kids far more entertainment than is healthy. I felt like I was showing them that life was meant to be lived in a chronic state of stress. That there is no natural way to achieve calm. That it can only be achieved with a screen or a substance. But I wanted to show them that being present and calm can be practiced in all moments of life (washing dishes, playing catch, walking, etc.).

Back in a state when some subtraction was needed, I began to search for what I could deduct. I looked at my tasks in order of importance. I had to work, take care of the family, and maintain my health. My spouse and I did a pretty good job of coordinating school drop-offs and pick-ups, organizing backpacks and lunches, dinner and chores, and dishing out a healthy balance of yes and no when the kids asked for things. I'd love to not do those, but easing my boys into those responsibilities is for another day. I didn't want to drop the things I loved. The activities that forced me to be present as a parent. Helping my kids put worms on hooks, playing endless wiffleball games, talking and learning about football, wrestling matches in the living room, and messy science experiments. Engaging in each other's interests had a positive impact on our family unit. Lastly, I looked at what extra tasks I may have taken on simply because of virtual peer pressure, access to online events, and extra tasks related to being online. What things did moms of the past not do? What activities did I sign the boys up for simply because I clicked on an advertisement? In my search, I discovered a lot.

Somehow, I had the belief that as the matriarch of the family, it was my job to post family updates online. I felt responsible to share our daily activities, vacations, special birthday and anniversary posts. I had an ah ha moment when I realized that my spouse could not care less about posting photos. I both look up to the way he lives and resent him for the ease in which he can shrug off things that hook me. Not once has he been told me that our family members enjoy seeing photos of the boys or of us online. It is not *expected* in any way that he be the one to post. In fact, he would be completely offline if we didn't have a small business. Ironically, when I took on the extra task to "influence" others to be active on Instagram, it made me inactive with my own children. Taking a photo or video stopped me from doing the very things I enjoyed the most with them: playing, throwing, tagging, running, kicking. Parents have always snapped photos of their family. But it didn't used to come with multiple steps. To keep snapping until I got the best shot. To post it and then tend to my phone to see who was liking it. Those little interruptions add up. The words older parents love to share kept ringing my ear: "It goes by fast."

We mistakenly copy each other's behavior. We see our friends post about all the events they're doing and what they're buying while ignoring being present with ourselves. I noticed the more I saw other moms' behavior online, the more I saw moms like that in life. The ones online always looked happy, but the ones in real life did not. It's even a persona to be a mom who "loves coffee." Scroll through several mom bloggers on Instagram, and you're bound to see it as their hashtag or tagline. Add to that "a lover of *target*." Are these the people we want to emulate? Are these the behaviors we want to copy?

Seeing advertisements for events and photos of what other parents are doing online pushes us to overschedule our kids. In truth, kids need a good deal of their time spent with family, unstructured, working through boredom. Instead, we say yes when someone texts us an invite to do that camp with their child. We overschedule their day and then reward them for their hard work with screen time. If too much screen time affects their learning, mental health, or sleep, we give them whatever "support" or supplement is trending. In turn, we look first to give them something to calm their anxiety instead of taking anything away. We don't think twice about this cycle because *everyone else is doing it*. I would search online for what I should be doing to be content. In actuality, I should have stopped searching at all. I looked for what I should be doing with my kids, my style, my time.

We appease kids with screens so we can get things done, thus never modeling for them how to do simple tasks, or to have them help do them. We have modern devices that even do things for us (dishwashers, etc.), but we don't use that extra time to be. Instead, we find something else to do. Scroll, watch TV, pop a pill. We don't need to buy (aka add) replacement toys for our kids to replace the screen. We just need to be with them. Adding something will never replace or fix that.

Email and messaging on smartphones give us tasks 24/7. Smartphones put everything at our fingertips. If you organize the family calendar, you are also the checker of sport's scheduling apps. You are the texter of getting and giving rides. It curated a habit of always doing something else when we are doing anything else. Our culture equates doing with efficiency. When I'm liking Facebook posts, answering emails, or responding to notifications in, say, a grocery store line, I think I'm being efficient. But if my goal is to be more present throughout the day, then what I'm doing in that moment is actually very inefficient. When we have the opportunity to be still, why not take that time to be present?

I found I was always looking for the answer online. Simplicity is a trending topic online and instead of just *being* , we are looking for things *to do* (declutter, paint walls white, meditate), and things to take ("calm" pills, supplements, anti-anxiety meds), instead of accepting what we are and how we feel. Do we need to be buying supplements when we could pause and be present with our negative emotions? What chance do the younger generations who observe us have if they see the way we handle (or rather not handle) our emotions?

Smartphones keep us from practicing mindfulness. They allow us to mask all of our feelings instead of being with them. When these devices didn't exist, walking to pick the kids up from school would've been just that, walking. These are the moments to be present. Instead, any extra moment in our day became a chance to be efficient. *I can send that last email while walking. I can log my fitness on the gym and nutrition app while making dinner*. There are some things that allow us to be more present than others (working out, walking, singing, playing games with kids). Instead of multitasking, it's better to do one thing at a time.

In the end, I graduated from this bout of therapy very quickly. My problem was no longer in my head. It was an external problem I had fixed again by subtraction. As a lasting message, my therapist told me to use these words a guide: "What does your soul want?" It stuck, and I no longer needed her services. For now, anyway.

PROTECT SIMPLICITY:

- ***Take breaks from digital media when your anxiety increases.*** Use negative emotions as a cue. Just as I realized it was time to take a break from caffeine, you can practice the same strategy with digital stressors. This can allow you to reset and come back with a healthier and non-automated approach as opposed to just being on the screen.

- ***Say no more often***. If it is not an automatic yes, then say no. As a former people pleaser, saying no felt uncomfortable at first. But I encourage you to trust your intuition. It is your mind's way of making it obvious what your soul actually wants.

- ***Fill your schedule with meaningful things.*** If you don't fill your schedule, the easiest, most dopamine-filled habits will fill it for you. I gained much more confidence in saying no when I took the initiative to schedule what I wanted to be doing first. I fill my schedule with activities aligned with my goals and values first, so there is less time to do undesirable things (for me which would be drinking or scrolling). Pay for things that will keep you accountable to your desired schedule. For example, I find value in paying for grocery delivery service, nutrition counseling, gym membership (if I didn't own the gym).

- ***Quit your perceived job of designated family photographer and social media poster***. I was already overexerting myself in the preparation of kids' activities, birthday parties, vacations, family get togethers, etc. I refused to disallow myself to enjoy the fruits of my labor. I stopped posting about such events. When events arrive, I ask others to share their photos, or I delegate someone else to document them.

- ***Delegate tasks to free your schedule.*** The term "play date" wasn't in my vocabulary when I was younger. It was just expected that the neighborhood kids would get together to play. Not all kids have neighbors, but mine do.

They also have legs and bikes. So I encourage them to knock on doors or give their friends' parents a call to help take the job of playdate-maker off my to-do list. Extracurricular activities come with the added task of checking online correspondence. I teach the family how to check game and practice schedules, what uniform color to bring, or how to sign up for bringing snacks.

- ***Take moments for yourself.*** There seems to be this push to always be doing something. When COVID-19 hit and we were forced to be at home, I did the things I want to now do every spring. I meditated in the sunlight from a chair in my garage. I took my kids for daily hikes at the nearby trail. That was living. Not this shuffle of buying and then stressing over buying too much stuff. Not this taking on of too many tasks, too many roles, and too much of shuffling our kids around. I decided that in memory of those simple days, instead of spring cleaning every year, I'm engaging in spring enjoying. I'm a resident of Michigan, so I'll be damned if such a long-awaited moment with a slightly warm breeze and half a day of sunshine is spent cleaning.

- ***Be cautious about adding more apps in the name of simplifying life.*** When I first started learning about meditation, I struggled to find the time and discipline to sit and breathe for even five minutes. I bought a meditation app, but it just became another task on my list. I ignored every reminder it sent. Instead, I've found the most success practicing mindfulness in everyday activities - washing dishes, putting away laundry, or walking without my phone are all simple ways to be present. My general rule is not to try to simplify life by adding yet another app. The more I use paper and pencil, or simply turn inward, the more at peace I feel.

Chapter 11

Unfollow Filling Up on Digital Candy

Digital vegetables can be a healthy use of screens (researching a term paper), while digital candy (Minecraft, Candy Crush) are hyperarousing and dopamine-activating digital stimulants without any ostensible health benefit.

—Nicholas Kardaras

Growing up with six siblings, we were by no means indulgent. We didn't have the money to be. With the typical "bad-for-you" things of the time, we weren't overly restricted. Soda pop and television was only moderately restricted. Our same-aged peers next door, however, had very restricted television programming and sugar allowance. Specifically, I recall they were only allowed to watch *Veggie Tales,* and their Kool-Aid was made with a quarter of the sugar. They would walk over and ask us to play. And while my siblings and I ran around outside, they mostly sat in front of our TV, binging on our soda pop and

Better Made potato chips. Sometimes our good intentions can backfire.

As CrossFit gym owners and athletes, my husband and I have been focused on fitness and nutrition for more than a decade. So I found the analogy of good technology use as nutritious food and bad technology use as non-nutritious food easy to understand. As with most things, however, understanding doesn't seamlessly transfer into implementation. In fact, it was one of the earliest lessons I learned while working on my bachelor's in psychology. My favorite professor, while educating us on social psychology, spoke of his four divorces. He taught me that understanding how we worked as humans would only go so far. We would have to work hard at any desire to change. I wanted our family to be more technologically nutritious. We had some rules here and there, but we needed to nail some things down. I would have to sell them on this analogy and tread lightly so it didn't backfire on me.

Every year, the morning after Halloween, my husband throws out 90 percent of the candy the kids spent hours collecting. It bothered me at first. They worked hard for that! But I know too much sugar consumption does more harm than good. If piles of candy are in front of any child, they will likely fill up on it and have little appetite for real food. So I allow him to throw it out and observe how they rarely notice. We are spared many chaotic moments as a result. We know that the risk in an evening ice cream cone is the kids spending wind-down time jumping on the sofas. I noticed an after-effect of too much sugar on myself as well, especially through alcohol. When I indulged in too many sugary treats, I felt light-headed, and even a little bit seems to cause an asthma flare-up. When consuming alcohol, it relieved stress in the moment but caused anxiety the next day.

Many similarities between actual sugar and digital sugar came to mind. It dawned on me how much our use of video games mimicked that of alcohol use. Both video games and alcohol were being used as my crutch. Alcohol was my aid to get through social situations. For years, I wouldn't even try going without a drink when I set foot at a social event. Video games were a crutch for when I wanted to get stuff done. They both seem to have the same positive quality: They bring people together to socialize. Besides that, neither provides any "nutritional" value.

One might argue that video games provide the benefit of developing problem-solving skills. However, that has not been my experience. In fact, it's been the opposite. I still remember the fights my brothers had over the PlayStation when I was a child. With my own children, I tried to rationalize that video games are like playing a sport. But if they acted the way they do on the Xbox at their baseball game, they would be pulled from the game.

We have to monitor, intervene, create plans, re-create plans, and put out fires. Their use rarely demonstrates they are learning any sort of problem-solving skills that will lead them to be model citizens.

Our pediatrician recommends a daily screen time limit of two hours. I know this guideline is important for young people with developing brains and bodies. Screens are full of tiny flashing images, some naked to the eye. They mess with our brains more than we know, possibly more than sugar. It causes stimulation overload. If we are following doctor's orders, in overusing tech for the bad stuff, we are leaving little time for the good stuff. Just as with our diets, if we are filling up on the bad food, we have less of an appetite for the good stuff.

What's hard is that when our kids are indulging in both sugary "food" and screen time, they appear content. They are getting little hits of dopamine. I believe we are, too, because when they are not complaining or fighting, we are generally more content too. Video game allowance reduces stress—dopamine for them, peace for me—until the fights, the crash, and the overstimulation aftermath cause more stress. We will always be exposed to non-nutritious foods, the same way we will be exposed to screens in a digital world. Perhaps it's about practicing moderation in a way that is healthy and responsible.

Every day we are thrown temptations. It is the world we live in. When we attend family or friend gatherings, the countertop usually has an array of decadent sweet treats, chips, and dips. An extra special dessert is usually presented at the end. I'm not going to ask my relatives not to have them. When I send the boys to a sleepover, I'm not going to disallow them to eat Doritos and cookies. Just as with food, I know that I cannot control what technology options will be present at others' homes. My youngest can sniff out video games and ice cream like no other. I can limit what I can in my own home, but when it comes to the availability of these things in the wild, I have to work at it in a different way. I can bring awareness to the costs and benefits of indulging in digital candy so that my children one day notice them on their own. I can model balance. In choosing to eat out at restaurants, we will nonetheless eat a mix of non-healthy and moderately healthy foods. We are not going to eliminate eating out entirely, just as we are not going to eliminate screens entirely.

PROTECT SIMPLICITY:

- ***Focus on the "good tech."*** I've always believed in the power of focusing on what to do verses what not to do. In my twenties, after I attempted to lose the college fifteen with SlimFast and calorie restriction, I found being hangry most days was not the way I wanted to live life. I decided to fill up on food I deemed as healthy. This worked well for me. I found that not long into this, I craved the good stuff, making my food choices even easier. Maybe I'm delusional, but I envision a not-so-distant future where my kids use devices mainly for digital vegetables. For this to happen, it's important to leave out appropriate devices for them to use. Positive reinforcement goes a lot further with my kids then barking at them or constantly saying no. I want them to freely pick these devices up and thrive. While aiming for pediatrician-recommended digital allowance of two hours per day, I want to prioritize digital vegetables—content that adds to well-being—within this time. For example, prioritizing activities that foster creativity and problem-solving, like using devices for music, audiobooks, research, or video creation. Using digital vegetables like simple digital watches, or flip phones for young children, confidently so as to influence others to do so as well. I don't want my children to continue growing up in a home of constant no's but of enthusiastic yeses.

- ***Make your smartphone dumb.*** Though many are moving to the use of "dumb phones," I've had some success with dumbing my current one down. This means removing apps down to the essentials and identifying which tasks are important enough to keep using the phone for. It removes temptations, and limits access to temptations: "out of sight, out of mind." When our home internet goes out, the work is done for us. On normal days, however, I have to physically remove temptations. Just as I am intentional with opening a bottle of wine (that I know we will have to finish the entire contents of), not purchasing too many unhealthy foods and keeping digital candy out of reach is important for limiting temptation. I can simplify choices by removing easy access to digital candy. For example, I hide or remove apps and games that are more distracting than beneficial.

- ***Use digital candy that bonds you***. I also want to encourage "digital candy" that bonds our family. Playing with filters on Snapchat, singing on the Smule app, and watching shows together on Netflix are all activities that let us have fun together. Limiting digital candy use for special occasions. Use the Xbox as a way to connect with others (with friends or on family game night).

- ***Find creative ways to get dopamine hits.*** Our brains crave novelty. My kids successfully replace the screen with more creative activities when they are ever-changing. Iron beads may work for one week, puzzles for another, and then they are on the hunt for something new. As an adult, I, too, jump between hobbies in search for that hit of dopamine. I store various activities, games, and toys and rotate their use to better engage them in those activities.

- ***Practice regular family screen breaks.*** We almost always had soda pop in our home growing up. I drank it pretty regularly. Slamming a can of Mountain Dew was a pretty common post-soccer practice refresher for me. I drank it through high school, specifically most days at 8:00 a.m. in geometry class. We also grew up Catholic, so every year when Lent rolled around, I chose this as the indulgence to give up for forty days. What I remember most is that every time I got past those forty days, I no longer wanted it. Breaks can recalibrate cravings toward healthier digital habits as well. The first time our family took an extended break from video game use, it took only four days for my kids to stop asking about it. Making technology breaks a family practice that includes everyone demonstrates that even adults benefit from the practice. Taking them regularly shows kids that they are simply a routine and there is nothing to fear. They can relax as we use the time to engage in non-digital activities that everyone enjoys, such as learning new card games, or playing board games that have been collecting dust.

- ***Remember that digital candy isn't love.*** Sometimes we get caught up thinking it is unloving to say no to certain things. That loving them means treating them with donuts, ice cream, iPads, and smartphones. Avoid associating these things with affection and love to maintain a healthy balance. While treating our kids can be enticing, tangible items are not a substitute for meaningful interaction.

- ***Teach intuitive digital consumption.*** It took me until I was in my late thirties to realize that the constant gas I had throughout my life could actually have been prevented. I am a pretty intuitive eater these days. If I had listened to my instinct earlier, it would have saved me a lot of pain and embarrassment. Intuition can be applied to our tech use as well. When I found my attention span plummeting following too many clicks on the Reddit app, I removed it from my phone. Discussing the impact of digital choices with my family goes a lot further than simply saying no, or "I told you so." I am working on encouraging them to reflect on how different digital activities make them feel to foster awareness and better decision-making.

Chapter 12

Unfollow Creativity Inhibitors

A discovery is said to be an accident meeting a prepared mind.

—Albert Szent-Gyorgyi

Forty-two messages notified me of their importance at band practice one night. As I was attempting to read lyrics off my phone, a banner popped up every other word. If I hadn't established this as my protected creative time, I'm pretty sure that evening would have been spent responding to messages. One notification check leads to another, and one app exploration leads to another, to another, to another. It's easy to see how scrolling has become many people's sole past time. Scrolling often prevents us from having enough creative motivation to even imagine other things to do with our time. I refuse to let staring at my phone be my hobby.

Don't you love how the universe sometimes throws out what you're itching for? When I moved to my current neighborhood, I discovered my neighbor across the street was a visual artist. The best part about this artist entering my life isn't that she gifted us with a 2'x4' portrait of our family. It's not that she taught me how to paint. And it's not that she watches our cats when we go on trips. It's that I get to observe a person who reaps the benefits of alone time. She produces beautiful things after spending hours on end madly enthralled in her craft. I know better than to compare myself to her. I've learned that doing so online is part of the reason social media makes me feel bad. Therefore I know not to do it in real life. My neighbor and I lead different lives. A woman close to eighty, she grew up in a different time. Her kids are grown. Nonetheless, she inspires me to live like she does. I needed some confirmation that it was okay to take some "me time." In that same universe-throwing-things-out-to-me way, a friend texted me something along the lines of the importance of engaging in hobbies. She told me about something called "Unicorn Time" that she's trying out from a book called *Fair Game* by Eve Rodsky. She described this Unicorn Time first as what it's *not:* "They say it's not social media, drinks with friends, mani/pedi, TV, reading, or attending a workout class." But she said, "You need a hobby or interest outside of being a mom or employee—sewing, skiing, interior decorating, music, etc.)." [1]

If you know me, you'll think I'm crazy trying to add more hobbies. Sure, I have the band and my CrossFit classes. But they still mimic obligations that may be inadvertently teaching my kids that we need to always be in go mode. It misses the point. Instead, I want them to see me fully enamored with a hobby (writing in a journal, drawing, singing, dancing). My passion for singing is better served with a sing-along in the car verses a stressful show. On the other end of the spectrum, CrossFit is fun and I love it, but it's more my lifeline than a hobby. I want to be engaged in hobbies for myself and for my kids in the hopes that they know that the joy of imagination doesn't end in young adulthood.

Getting to a flow state is my favorite. Sometimes I become so engrossed in it I can get myself in trouble—forgetting to prep dinner or put the clothes in the dryer. But it is worth it when the end product is a creation of my own doing. I know when my kids are in a flow state. My oldest whistles, my middle child hums, and my youngest doesn't ask to play video games. Life is so fulfilling in those moments we forget about the screen. But it happens less often than I'd like. There are just too many other shiny options fighting for our attention. There is a reason many tech execs have disallowed screen-use for their children.

In the '80s and '90s, my friends and I jumped from creative venture to creative venture. We utilized the technology available to us. Hours were spent recording silly news skits with my friend's dad's hulky camcorder. Thousands of photos were taken and processed when we played "Glamour Shots," which gave us basic training in photography. Much time and attention was spent on lighting, costuming, and backdrop placement. The thrill from awaiting photos to be processed was unmatched. My brother and I created a pretty sophisticated faux newsletter on our desktop computer. Thirty years later and I still practice the same creativity. If given the option, we surely would have posted our ventures for likes, clout, and money. I feel lucky to have not had the option. Even when I began sharing my writing as an adult via a blog, I found my creativity impacted by what I feared my audience might think. It ended up killing my creative energy.

I want my kids to experience their own creative ventures with the appropriate use of technology as well. There are amazing tools that can enhance our creativity. But with cameras, music, and phones brought to us in a one-stop shop, it's difficult to utilize devices solely for the purpose we set out to use them for. Just as my good intentions are often disrupted by notifications, I know that my children's will be too. How can we prevent scrolling and virtual messaging from becoming our only hobby?

PROTECT SIMPLICITY:

- ***Assign devices for creative use only.*** Assigning an old iPhone to a child as a "music player" dedicated to creative pursuits can demonstrate the potential of technology as a tool for creativity. To maintain focus on creativity, remove app stores from devices like iPads and iPhones used for specific purposes. This setup minimizes distractions and encourages the use of technology for creative ventures only. Technology enhances creativity when used wisely.

- ***Get adequate exposure to nature.*** Integrating nature into daily routines can stimulate creativity. For example, announcing outdoor recess time during the summer encourages my kids to continue explorations, such as science experiments learned at camp, fostering a deeper connection with the natural world and sparking creative thinking.

- ***Schedule creative time.*** Incorporating what I call "forced creativity" into a schedule ensures regular engagement with the creative process. Joining a band for weekly practice sessions provides a structured environment where creativity is essential. This approach can also be applied to my kids by introducing them to new projects, like painting or sculpting, to nurture their creative development.

- ***Make prearranged creative spaces and stock them with the right tools.*** I think about how many fewer artists or musicians there could be in the future, if children today aren't bored enough to tinker with or explore various talents and skills. I picture myself as a child, a preteen, and a teen hanging out with my best friends, making creative things because we had to figure out how to spend our time. I picture what that would be like if we were given smartphones from our parents back then. We would simply be staring at screens next to our friends, just as we do next to our siblings and our family today. I see all the creativity that has been denied. It's why the creators of these things don't let their own kids use them. Building an environment where creative activities are easily accessible can help bypass the allure of digital screens. Organizing spaces for activities like Legos, Play-Doh, and board games, increasing the likelihood that kids will engage with them. Regularly changing crafts to keep them novel can also help maintain interest.

- ***Turn off notifications.*** During creative activities, turning off notifications on your devices can help maintain focus. Setting specific times to check messages and communicating this to family and friends ensures uninterrupted creative sessions while still being responsive to urgent needs.

- ***Explore real-life hobbies.*** Avoiding excessive screen time by exploring and practicing real-life hobbies ensures that these activities remain more appealing than digital scrolling. Pick one thing to experiment with for a week and see how it feels. If you enjoy it, you're set! If not, be grateful for the experience you had and try something else the next week. My hope is for my kids to develop a wide range of creative skills while preventing a reliance on digital devices for entertainment.

Chapter 13

Unfollow Validation Addiction

If you need somebody else to tell you that you are special, then you have not done anything to earn it in your own mind.

—Shwetabh Gangwar

My niece's arrival to a Christmas party has always stuck with me. The first words out of the seven-year-old's mouth weren't "Merry Christmas" or "Hello" when she arrived. They were, "Did you give me a *like* on my YouTube video?" Smartphones and social media came around about the time she was born, which was also when I became an aunt. I had no kids of my own, nor was I working in elementary education yet. Therefore, my first observations of raising a family in the digital age was of my older brother and his family.

Unlimited and unfiltered use of social media apps was the norm in their household. I observed my niece grow addicted to online attention quicker than the average kid. Within a couple of years, still under age eleven, she had thousands of followers on

Musical.ly (now TikTok). Though some may see this as a success, I knew it wasn't.

Thinking back to when my firstborn was seven, I'm grateful to reflect on a different scenario. A video of him dancing was shared from his dance studio on Facebook. When I showed him, his immediate response was not, "How many likes did I get?" He didn't even know what Facebook was, nor could he conceptualize the idea of strangers and friends caring about a video of him. He didn't care much for it himself. Instead, upon seeing it, he was reminded of how much he loved dancing. He immediately busied himself by setting up a dance party in the basement. My son had yet to experience the addiction of gaining validation in an online world. I hope he never does.

It is human nature to seek validation. As a middle child, I didn't grow out of the need for my parent's approval until I was well into my thirties. Like most of us, I will always crave it to some extent. I want to know that what I do, what I say, and who I am matters. Posting online is effective in generating responses from people. There seems to be little shame in bragging on social media, too, be it humble or not. It's even considered odd not to flaunt your best side. I found that seeking online affirmation was the gateway drug to other tech habits I was trying to unfollow. I made the decision to be mindful of how I was seeking validation and from whom. Whenever I felt the urge to post online for the sake of praise, attention, and likes, I stopped myself. And let me tell you, it wasn't easy.

I had to get comfortable with the loneliness that comes from relying on self-validation versus outward validation. Part of this process meant being okay with watching others receive the attention we so naturally crave. It also meant accepting that others may not see the hard work you put in. By posting minimally—say, only for promotion—you gain little to no acknowledgement for the work happening behind the scenes. I wanted to post the cool things I did, too, so everyone could see how hard I worked. But simply recognizing that desire reminded me how important it was to stick to my guns and refrain.

I had to silence my fear of missing out on the opportunity for little dopamine hits of praise. The opportunity for the oohs and ahhs in revealing daily achievements. I was overcome with fear-based questions: *What's the point of going somewhere great if people don't reinforce how awesome and adventurous my life is? Am I really beautiful, athletic, and successful if friends and strangers online don't say so in likes, emojis, and positive comments? How can I be happy if others don't know how awesome I am?*

I had to accept that I might be rejected by some for not regularly sharing about my life online and responding to their posts with enthusiasm. I told myself a story that others would question if I was happy in my life because I wasn't bragging about it on social media. I told myself they would forget about me entirely, and that it mattered if they did. Now I tell myself the story that I am awesome, and I don't care who knows it.

I almost convinced myself to get back in the swing of posting about what I did to *influence* others to live deliberately and actively. But as much as that could be true, I simply couldn't find it in me to do so when such an incredibly large part of my own deliberate living is limiting how much I am online. I could not honestly say I was working toward greatness, or living intentionally, if I was using a technological device to feed my need for validation. My absence on the socials just might be far more influential than anything I could post.

PROTECT SIMPLICITY:

- ***Limit how much you post on social media***. I crave that quick fix of validation like the rest of us. Avoiding bragging on what a friend called "Brag book" can be very difficult. I'm a middle child after all! This is my main motivation against posting. It's not that posting causes severe damage. But for me, it's about practicing habits that help me work toward the person I want to be. I don't want to be hooked on what I do or what I have and throwing it out for others to see, in turn creating a constant stream of seeking approval. I don't want to be dependent on external validation. I want self-validation. It is an uncomfortable feeling to opt out of receiving the attention that you observe others getting. It's even more difficult knowing that posting photos of yourself doing cool things isn't that bad. But the validation chase isn't in your blueprint of your best self. If you do have to post for promotional reasons, limit how much you check statuses on likes and comments. Delegate posting and any engagement if needed, and if possible.

- ***Love yourself regardless of external approval.*** I found that by ignoring the impulse to seek online validation, I reduced my need for it in the "real world" too. This means doing the things I love for me and no one else. It means being confident that I am a great parent, athlete, and friend, and stopping short of bragging about it online, just to be sure. In quitting the online persona—hardworking, athletic, near-perfect mom—only now do I feel remotely close to being that person. Though I work out, write, and am a parent, those things don't define me. When self-doubt creeps in, ask yourself, *What would I tell a close friend if they were feeling this way?* We are often kinder to others and can benefit from taking our own advice.

- ***Ask some key questions before you post on social media.*** To prevent myself from halting wonderful moments with my husband, kids, family, and even myself, I ask myself some questions before I post: *Will stopping my kids for this photo op make them feel good? Does posting this set me back today because I have to stop and look at how many people liked it? Who is this photo serving? Who will it impress? Is sharing this photo, writing, or comment within my personal values? Is this best-self behavior approved? Is it part of the identity I am trying to keep? Do I want a happy existence, or do I want the appearance of one?*

- ***Don't give in to peer pressure.*** We think of this as something that only happens to young people. But as adults, we are very much at risk of ignoring our own values for the sake of doing what others are encouraging us to do or are doing around us. In staying true to our own intuition, values, and purpose we can empower others to do so as well.

- ***Share via stories on accounts dedicated to projects.*** Sharing via stories has been a good way to share projects that can inspire others to try new things, or as a way to promote your business and different ventures. Stories are a quick way to share and provide less temptation to go back and check *likes*. There is no scripting, just snapping a photo or video and sending.

- ***Celebrate each win intentionally.*** I don't want my achievements' value tied to how many people acknowledge them. I prefer to celebrate in meaningful ways. Rather than automatically posting to a large audience, I find creative ways to honor my achievements. Choosing small groups to celebrate with is often far more meaningful.

- ***Avoid social comparison by scaling down the platforms you use via regular social media breaks***. Schedule in regular breaks that will allow you to reassess which social media platforms may be causing social comparison. Remove apps from your phone or bookmarks. Then, reassess which platforms to add back. You may find that seemingly innocent platforms, like Venmo or fitness trackers, may be causing you to compare your life, or your own progress, to others. They may have to be tweaked or removed to avoid sneaky social comparison. You may also find that in breaking from certain platforms, you develop a revulsion toward them.

Chapter 14

Unfollow Buying It

It's not having what you want, it's wanting what you've got.

—*Sheryl Crow*

I spent an entire Saturday of my existence the other day clearing clutter. This particular day I focused on clearing my kids' clothing. I had made an appointment for the following Tuesday at a consignment shop, so I had a deadline that helped immensely. In the clearing of closets of three children under age eleven, I found fifteen plaid shirts. I have spent the last several years hoarding this particular type of shirt because I've been conditioned that plaid shirts are a must for fall. Minus the single time I dressed (eh hem, *posed*) them in plaid shirts, they have not worn them. Luckily, I have come far from seven-years-ago me (when I was pregnant with my youngest), who posted pics of my kids for clout.

Back then, I could dress them up in whatever outfits I wanted to show them off in. They now have opinions on what they want to wear. What they choose on any given day—no matter the weather—are T-shirts (usually ones with the collar worn out, a stain or three, and a hem with a string hanging out). If it's not a T-shirt, it is a long-sleeved shirt, surprisingly in much better condition. Finally, despite my many attempts to send them out with a jacket, they reject them. Instead, rotating between one or two sweatshirts and two to four pairs of holey shorts and sweatpants. Needless to say, they have never chosen a plaid shirt. They have also never chosen to obey me when I told them to wear one. Not for Christmas, not for an apple orchard outing, not for warmth on a crisp autumn day.

I laugh thinking about the boys' unworn plaid shirts that will cheerfully fill the consignment shop. I think of how I am releasing myself of the 2000-pound weight of those fifteen shirts. I feel relieved to know that I will no longer accept or add the clothing that society makes me feel is necessary. And I look forward to the photos we will enjoy from a Christmas morning of *unmatched pjs* and awkward poses—just like my childhood.

I've been wasteful too many times during my limited days on Earth. Hypnotically purchasing unneeded items and gifting my future self with the hassle of getting rid of them in the process. I made a commitment that Saturday to not be in this same situation again. I started to work to buy less so I could gain more of anything but stuff and the stress that came with it. In my newfound practice of unfollowing, I accept, even embrace, our family not "dressing the part." In dropping the notion that I needed to present ourselves to others in a certain way, I found the freedom to not buy into a practice that was essentially buying things for others.

Freedom also came with not posting for all the occasions. I very rarely post "obligatory" photos for first days of school, holidays, seasonal events, and so on. If and when we go to an apple orchard next, I won't post about it. This takes away any pressure I used to put on myself to dress the family up in cutesy autumn-inspired outfits. It takes away the need to stop them from exploring the orchard to have them pose until the shot is right.

It helped me pull myself from the consumerism trap that said I needed to buy them trendy clothing. Not only is there enough to go around via donations or resale shops, but it also allows them to be in charge of their own self-expression. I don't force my kids to wear clothes that will look good to others but serve no functional purpose. They are allowed to be and express themselves as the active individuals they are. Family and friends who see them love them no matter what, eager to dish out hugs and kisses, not likes and comments. And though they would no doubt look cute if their outfits were the latest fashions, or at the very least matching, I'm not sure I'd be seeing their sweet little personalities shine through. Unsurprisingly, their peers love and respect them anyway for who they are. Overall, this freedom allows them to be who they are, not who I want others to perceive them as.

Spending less time living on the digital grid is good for your wallet. When you're not constantly influenced, you can be in more control of how and when you are spending. You miss out on many of the current trends. This was on par with my mission to be un-trending. Call me crazy, but busy schedules, too much stuff, and buying into the revolving door of brands just stopped appealing to me.

Sitting at breakfast at a Hampton Inn in mid-Michigan, I saw the tween soccer players roll in first. Next came the recognizable look of a forty-something mom, complete with black Lululemons, Nike kicks, an oversized sweatshirt, a pastel Stanley cup with a straw, and a crossbody bag. (This was, of course, weeks before Stanleys were dropped for Owalas.) Though the hotel offered free coffee, the ensemble was complete with a Starbuck's coffee. On my way back to the room, I saw the costume again in the elevator. I almost believed it was the same group of women, but I noticed slight alterations: a silver Stanley sippy, a black tank top, Nike ball cap, and lip injections. I wanted to purge the desire to morph into everyone around me. It perturbed me that I subconsciously desired to emulate how these women had put themselves together. It seems that I, along with many others, are often put under a spell that makes us click the purchase button. I decided I might rather be untrendy than continue to be caught up in it all.

I think we mistakenly believe *coolness* for ourselves and our kids is linked to what we wear, where we live, what we own, and what we buy. We seem to have evolved to thinking sameness is cool and uniqueness is not. Perhaps we start out by attempting to stand out, but we feel a kinship to fitting in as well. We don't even realize that in an attempt to be unique, we all start to look the same. Our homes are almost identical inside and out, and our kids are all rocking the same apparel. I have found myself, a grown woman, buying stuff to feel cool. We as a society have adopted a "more is better mindset," yet we feel worse than we've ever.

We convince ourselves we need that thing, and if that doesn't work, we tell ourselves we deserve it. We have an unending thirst for more. And not solely a thirst for *stuff.* We have a thirst to hold on desperately to youth, to validate that we are important, and to fit in while we try to stand out (as someone with the most money, someone who is the happiest, someone who has it all.). Exuding coolness, though, is not in what we buy or wear or even in what activities we do. Coolness is related to authenticity. It's how good we are at being our authentic selves. The final straw for me was when the holidays stopped feeling joyful. Working through the trifecta of Halloween-Thanksgiving-Christmas felt like working toward an extra career. Seeing holiday decor pop up in stores caused more dread than when school supplies arrived.

With each year there seems a new socially instilled tradition: the sending of holiday cards, matching family pajamas, Elf on the Shelf, and cookie decorating—to project the perfect image, either to the kids or our social media accounts. When I saw gingerbread houses sold as a Valentine's activity, it felt like a new low. Was any holiday spared from the need to consume and entertain? I put my new focus toward what could bring joy to me and my family. I worked to buy less in order to gain more.

PROTECT SIMPLICITY:

- ***Buy less new and more pre-owned.*** These days, there is more than ever at "gently used" shops. With an overabundance of stuff, people look for ways to get rid of their clutter. I often find that what I purchase has never been used. In shopping at specific consignment stores, I find that they only accept the latest fashions. Therefore, when I am on the hunt for a specific item, I can rest assured that I will find what I am looking for. There is not a need to be on Instagram in order to keep up.

- ***Commit to buying stuff that will last, and limit how much you buy of it.*** I recently caught myself in a splurge that I regretted immediately. As the items arrived, I realized they were all plastic. Even the "wood" item I got. I realized they would last three years tops. And if they lasted longer than that structurally, they wouldn't last aesthetically. I returned all the items that weren't perishable or hygiene products. And I committed right then and there to only make purchases for things if they will last. Before I buy something, I will research for a higher quality item.

- ***Put extra thought into each purchase.*** I think about them for a while. I also make sure there is a space for said thing and that it is something we will actually use. I am mindful about purchasing something I already have that fills that purpose. When we got to the point in our society where a water bottle was accepted as a fashion accessory, or rather, a status accessory (not just for adults but children as well), I knew it was time to stop following the trends. I make an effort not to overdo it with water bottles, as I already have enough to fill the purpose they would serve for me – drinking water on the go. With each purchase, I'm asking myself, *Is this going to end up broken in the trash in three weeks? When we are gifting cheap, plastic toys, aren't we actually just gifting them a future of Earth cleanup?* If I'm going to acquire items, I want at least some of them to pass the test of time.

- ***Avoid appeasing your discontent with consumption.*** It is easy to get caught in a habit of solving discontent with consumption. We have the ability to consume content via technology 24/7. We are more influenced than ever to consume *stuff.* Our phones are always with us, readily available to provide us escape. If our social media and email accounts don't tempt us with purchasing things to make us feel better about ourselves, we need look no further than those around us. Take the time to find more fulfilling hobbies and endeavors than consumption. Don't allow consumption to be your hobby. Assess your day. Are you stuck in a cycle of working and consuming? Branch into more fulfilling activities that involve creating, moving, and learning, and observe how much freer you feel. Movement is medicine for your mind. Feed your mind good information. What you consume mentally affects your mental state. Replace doom-scrolling with content that teaches you something valuable.

- ***Practice acceptance, mindfulness, and gratitude during the holidays.*** There is a lot I want to remove from my family's holiday experience (an overabundance of stuff, a large hole in the checking account, my young ones' feelings of discontent until they have more). But it's really more about what I want to add to the experience. First, I am working on practicing acceptance that my children will forever receive gifts that will clutter our home. That means being okay with friends and family giving in their own way. Though gifts of "experiences" are preferred, I will not deny my loved ones the joy it may bring them to give tangible items. In addition, with any experience gift I give, I include a small tangible item and a photo of the experience, or I stretch out the gift-giving process by creating a scavenger hunt. Next, I'm practicing mindfulness so the moments stay within me and my boys. The Christmas season itself should be the experience. So much so that an overabundance of presents isn't needed to make up for any lack of good experience. I have fond memories as a child of opening a few presents that I really, really liked. Besides that, the Christmas memories I cherish most are singing carols with my siblings under the street light, exchanging gag gifts of items found in our basement, eating a big breakfast, listening to music on the record player, drinking a warm beverage, lazing in pajamas all day, sitting by a cozy fire, and singing my favorite hymns at Mass. The more I implement traditions not tied to acquiring things, the more likely my children are to feel empowered to buy less in their future. Because if I don't change, at least just a little, when will the cycle end? Lastly, I'm practicing gratitude for all that I am able to offer and contribute in the holiday season. If I hadn't stopped and reflected on why I was stressed holiday after holiday, I would have mistakenly continued to buy more and more in an attempt to make it more enjoyable.

- ***When you enter the digital world to make a purchase, go in with a plan.*** I refuse to buy more than I would have if technology wasn't a thing. If online stores didn't exist, I wouldn't be buying random stuff to be sent to me the next day. What is masked as "convenience" for the consumer is really just convenience for the company. They make it really easy for people to spend endless amounts of money. I know that the minute I enter any webpage, check my email, or open any social media app, I will be thrown images of personalized ads with a genius sense of urgency. So, I prepare myself in a couple ways. I make a list early in the year and save up. Instead of being guided by faux "limited" sales, I am guided by an intentional list. With a list, I can buy months in advance of impending holidays or birthdays, allowing me to enjoy them more. In addition, I am prepared with a few good questions before I purchase anything deemed necessary. *Will I be tasked with having to get rid of this in a year? Do I have something similar in my home already? Will the excitement of this item last longer than Christmas morning?*

- ***Use digital media instead of it using you***. Many apps and services collect and utilize data for various purposes, including targeted advertising. Using burner emails or privacy-focused browser extensions can help limit your data footprint. I like to use digital media to my advantage and then clear my data. In our search for a new couch, I discovered that I could use social media to my advantage. I didn't want to dedicate a whole Pinterest board to the venture. For some reason, that app robs my creative energy instead of sparking it. It leaves me overwhelmed. Instead, I did a search for a new modular couch on Facebook. Then I waited a few hours. I picked a time to sit down, opened my web browser, and browsed through the handful of couch ads I had been sent. I found one, purchased it, and cleared my browser. I learned another method to take control of ads. One day I clicked on an ad for dog food that had shown up in my feed. I don't have a dog, but I was interested in reading through the comments. This sparked my feed to be full of ads for dog supplies. I'm never going to buy that stuff, so it's essentially like I removed the ads that were targeting me. Be mindful of data privacy and tracking.

- ***Unsubscribe to memberships at companies.*** We recently canceled our membership at a popular online shopping site. For a recent purchase, I also opted out of paying for shipping and selected the free option. Our package took forever to arrive. It was great, like old times. It works for the same reason removing social media apps from my phone works; it removes impulsivity in any actions I am trying to avoid.

Chapter 15

Unfollow Risky Behavior

Yesterday I was clever so I wanted to change the world.

Today I am wise so I'm changing myself.

—Rumi

I am a firm believer that someone, something—God, an angel, my own spirit, a deceased love one—sends me messages. A message I received once seemed pretty clear to me. It reminded me of why I'm sharing any of my thoughts on the digital world at all. If you are going to read any of this book, read this chapter. I believe it can help us all make better decisions and that the lesson wasn't just meant for me, but for me to share.

It was one of those rare seventy-degree days in Michigan. Seventy-two degrees to be exact. I was driving down the country road I enjoy taking on my way back from grocery shopping. I enjoy the stark difference the drive provides from the bustling area of the shopping center. I was full of ambition. I had gotten my shopping done, the school term had just begun, and the family would be arriving home soon from a trip. I had a lot on my to-do list so that I could present the family with a clean and organized home as we began the school week upon their return. I wanted a good song, so I picked up my phone to choose one. Luckily, I looked up, because a woman was walking on the side of the road about a quarter mile in front of me, seemingly doing the same thing—enjoying the weather and looking down at her phone to choose a great song to set as her soundtrack to this beautiful afternoon. I thought about how miles before I had swerved several times as I changed songs, made voice reminders to myself, and plugged my phone in.

I let my brain imagine the repercussions of hitting her. I thought first of the impact of my life. How I'd scream to myself, "No! No! Why did I do that?! Why did I care about a song at that moment? Why did that happen?!" I imagined myself calling my husband and saying, "There was an accident. I hit someone. They didn't make it." It felt so real. How I would look down at my lap at the cell phone on it in shame. How the cops would look at it without surprise. The words *distracted driver* popped in my head. Selfishly, I thought of the woman next. First with anger. *Why was her head down in her phone?* My friend, a runner, had taught me to always be aware of drivers and never trust them. It was the same thing I taught my kids anytime they were around the road. I thought of how her life would be over. How we would always be tied in some way. How I would have to face her family. All she wanted to do was take a walk. Overall, I felt grateful it hadn't happened to us this time. And how I had the privilege to drive into my garage and go back to my normal life, never to know or impact that individual. But some don't have it so lucky. And these moments happen in an instant as a result of the poor judgment you didn't even know you were making.

In the moments after I passed this woman, I threw my phone in the backseat right then and there. I vowed to change my routines ever so slightly so that this would be my new norm. For myself, to demonstrate to my family, and to let others know that sometimes we simply can't trust ourselves, so the phone will remain in a designated spot no matter how inconvenient. I'm just grateful all life lessons don't have to come from a tragedy.

I've heard that with parenting, little kids bring little problems, and big kids bring big ones. Though my little kids keep me pretty busy, I still find time to worry about what risky behaviors my big kids could one day venture into. When it comes to technology, there is no shortage of what parents can worry about. Distracted driving can have immediate and disastrous repercussions. Social media addiction, excessive screen use, porn sites, and inappropriate content viewing can be silent killers. I know that preventing these things will require strategies beyond parental control.

As a fitness professional, I feel it is appropriate to add sedentary lifestyle to risky living. Katy Bowman, author of Rethink Your Position, stresses that our bodies are designed for movement. She advocates for small movements throughout the day for big impact.[1] We are only beginning to see the impacts our new, and unnatural postures are starting to have on us.

PROTECT SIMPLICITY:

- ***Have a cue to remind yourself to hide your phone.*** Leave a map on your dashboard to remind yourself you only need your phone there if you are using it for navigation. If the phone in view is too tempting, set up navigation to audio so you can hear where you are going. Keep your phone in a designated spot in the car when you drive, and plan accordingly. Create a playlist of music before you start driving and put the phone out of sight. This means not multitasking on your phone in front of young people. Young people don't need any additional influence to drive distracted. If they see their parent drive distracted, they may become desensitized to the danger in it. Young eyes are always watching us. At home, have those with smartphones keep a book or journal next to their bed, or wherever they put their phone, so they can pick that up instead.

- ***Use driving as a time to practice mindfulness.*** Our home is in between the schools and a small-town downtown area, so we get a good amount of traffic. I once wrote a piece about how stopping at stop signs has hidden benefits after I noticed an influx of drivers breezing by them. I wrote about how not only is it a good opportunity to be a good neighbor, but it's a great time to take a cleansing breathe. Driving is a great time to breathe and reflect. Practicing mindfulness while driving can certainly help with road rage!

- ***Use technology that prompts you to move throughout the day.*** Engage in two good habits at once by listening to an audiobook while you walk. Put on some running shoes and a good playlist, and let the tempo motivate you towards jogging. Store your smartphone in your tennis shoes when you get home to encourage an "only use when moving" routine.

- ***Assure basic needs are not being hindered by a screen.*** Studies demonstrate that losing sleep due to increased screen use may be adding to mental health issues.[2] Don't sleep with your phone. Use an alternate alarm clock. Put focus into assuring basic needs like hygiene, nutrition, and sleep are being met.

- ***If another parent jumps off a bridge, don't jump off of it too.*** Don't let the reason you buy your preteen a smartphone be because everyone else is doing it. Know your child's individual needs and goals, and analyze how a smartphone may impact them specifically. When you do give them one, help them find it a home. Teach them that at their age they do not need to carry it with them everywhere. Provide parameters for its use.

- ***Guide your kids toward solutions.*** When challenges arise, I steer my children toward finding solutions rather than eliminating the problem. Encouraging creative solutions to boredom instead of relying on screens empowers them to become independent problem-solvers. The hope is that when bigger problems arise we can work together to find a solution.

- ***Practice the 20-20-20 rule.*** I was taught this rule by both my eye doctor and my physical therapist. For every 20 minutes spent at a screen, take a 20 second break, to view something 20 feet away. This is meant to reduce eye strain as well as reduce negative impacts from bad posture.

Chapter 16

Unfollow Inauthentic Living

Your core values are the deeply held beliefs that authentically describe your soul.
—John. C. Maxwell

When photo filters became a thing years ago, they were creativity-inducing and often silly. It seems around 2018 is when Instagram posts began shifting from ultra-filtered-but-in-a-silly-way to more perfected ones. If you take a very, very long scroll through an active poster's account, you will more than likely find these photos. They weren't attractive but they were fun. Today, many of the recommended accounts thrown at us have a similar look and much of the same content.

When I tried my hand as an influencer, the one thing that eluded me was authenticity. I think I know why. It's because perfection sells. The unpretty photos didn't get the likes. Once you are caught in the web of gathering likes and comments, you start to care about them. The natural progression of Instagram blogging is to morph it into what viewers are clicking on. Before you know it, you transform into a different identity, at least in the virtual way. Never did I share a photo or video of me losing my temper with my kids while working on that post. And I never saw any behind-the-scenes posts of others doing the same. Sadly, as seen with the story of Ruby Franke, the mission is to appear good, leaving not much time and energy to work on actually being good.

I have to wonder, can what we see online ever truly be authentic when the virtual world is a stage? Is it always social media versus reality? Can it ever be both? I recall at a young age, when Seventeen and YM magazines were my sources for advice. Even before Photoshop was a household tool, I knew that these weren't real women. The images produced unattainable standards for young people in search of an identity. Even more so, it led me to feeling bad for celebrities in the spotlight. I remember thinking, I never want to be famous. I never considered being an actress or pop star. I somehow knew that stardom would lead to trouble. Perhaps this is why showcasing myself online feels so uncomfortable to me.

A virtual presence seems to mimic stardom. Being "online" is essentially "being famous" —at least in your own little-big social media community. What I dislike about stardom is that it requires work to uphold an image. Once famous, you no longer have the freedom to be imperfect. If you are, then your audience's attention moves on to the next big thing. In the battle of social media versus reality, how could reality ever win? If you want the likes and the *shares* and the *followers*, you have no choice but to show your most perfect self. And with all the availability of online tools, how could we not be tempted to show that self? When people, "our fans," reinforce that more perfect self, why would we ever want to show our true self again?

The addiction to online attention is strong. I've been lured into the draw of the virtual spotlight before. Instagram seemed the worst at drawing me into this fantasy land. Many of the posts seem to follow the same formula, driving users to post the latest trend. We are guided by what draws the most attention. Once I received that attention, it magically mimicked true joy that I didn't even realize it was just vanity. When we showcase an altered reality, social media reinforces it by way of engagement. That attention makes the truth matter less, and what gains the most attention matter more. When it's social media versus reality, reality loses time and time again. The more success we have with our altered self, the more addicted we become to showing it.

I found the posting of skewed reality so interesting that for fun, I coined a new term for it: *Virtual Irony*. There are many types of irony. Some are immediately led to Alanis Morissette's words: "meeting the man of my dreams and then meeting his beautiful wife." But as a high school educator, I'm familiar with different types. Dramatic irony, for instance, is when the audience knows something that a character does not, say in a book or movie. This sticks out to me when I think of the virtual world. But not because it is what I observe. I observe the complete opposite. Since it didn't have a name, I gave it one. I think *Virtual Irony* is a great way to define when a character (aka our social media persona) knows something that the audience does not. Our social media persona knows the *truth* but shares something different. I'd simplify it by calling what we sometimes post of and about ourselves a big, fat lie, but it's much more creative than that. We may not even know when we are doing it.

Here are some examples:

- *The stressed-out parent who posts all the great moments with the kids. The audience chimes in with, "You're a great mom!" but she knows she's stressed out of her mind and ignored the kids to take the photos.*

- *The broken relationship that posts for anniversaries and family photos. The "character" knows something the "audience" does not: They are one counseling session away from splitting up.*

- *Posting about a personal or divisive topic with a secret agenda. The audience thinks you're sharing for the sake of sharing, but the persona knows they are sending a message to a specific individual.*

- *Posting heavily filtered photos to mask insecurities, creating an audience that may even be envious of their looks and confidence.*

- *Posting photos while having a lousy time. We care less about changing our circumstances and more about making sure our audience thinks we are having fun.*

It's time to come to peace with your relationship online. If you find yourself projecting someone else and are okay with it, that's great. If you find yourself feeling bad because you notice the façade, then it's time to alter it. For me, being all-in online gave me that "famous person" complex I didn't want. It distracted me from living in the moment. It also halted my growth because I focused solely on the growth of my feed instead of growing as a person.

PROTECT SIMPLICITY:

- ***Live with purpose.*** The key to the good life is getting to spend time expressing your talents. I was asked to join my current band smack dab in the middle of youth baseball season (balancing three different schedules). Not to mention while I was writing this book. So I asked myself: *Is joining the band worth it?* What if I was told I had little time left to live? I would still do it. In fact, it is the thing I would do, along with the other things I'm doing (watching the kids excel at sports, supporting them in their growth and learning, and playing with them in their activity of choice). I'd still do CrossFit because the side effect of working out is feeling good. I enjoy the challenge and sport of it, as well as the camaraderie of the classes. It's why I continued doing it through all my pregnancies. It's also important to live out my personal passions of writing, singing, parenting, and taking risks to stay true to myself in a world full of increasing influence.

- ***Mindfully engage with AI and algorithms.*** Recognize that algorithms shape the information you consume and can potentially limit your perspective. I am careful to continue the practice of critical thinking, so I maintain a questioning mindset toward AI-driven suggestions and information. As I use technological tools, I want to assure that I am not slowly morphing away from my own human thought process.

- ***Remove devices from interactions with other people.*** When I am meeting a friend for coffee, but also tending to my phone, I am not truly existing with that person. When I am with someone, distraction-free, I can have a truly authentic experience with them.

- ***Reject anything that blocks your soul.*** What if I was told I had little time left to live? What would I change about my life? When our bodies perish, I believe we are left with our souls. I am on a mission as if in a video game to deter what blocks my soul and add what feeds it, what allows it to shine, and to connect with others.

- ***Don't use technology to spread negativity or hatred.*** Words matter. When I was a server at a restaurant, a customer told me I was a ray of sunshine. I also think of the time a teacher called me absentminded. Both of those occurred more than thirty years ago, and I still think of them. The same goes for texting. Opting out of adding to text messages that speak badly of others is something I dropped long ago. I often refer back to words from Mother Teresa: "If you judge people, you have no time to love them." The digital age provides a quick avenue for releasing anger or tension. But not much good seems to come from posting, texting, or emailing negatively to or about others. It's best to stop and think, and perhaps call or talk to someone in person first. I like to follow the rule that if I wouldn't say it to someone's face, I won't say it behind their back.

- ***Don't pretend to be someone you're not.*** When I posted incessantly online, I was pretending to be an extrovert. During the pandemic, one thing I enjoyed about quarantine was not having to say no to invitations—the invites simply stopped. As an introvert, I loved that. I relish the joy of missing out online and am content knowing the real world satisfies me. Spend less time comparing yourself to others and more time appreciating your own strengths. When posting, resist the urge to present an altered version of yourself. Stand out from AI filters by sharing genuine, human moments in your photos.

Chapter 17

Unfollow Irresponsible Parenting

Behind every great child is a parent pretty sure they are

screwing it up.

Movies and television shows must have given me this imagery: The arrival of dusk on a summer evening, a swarm of lightning bugs, and little kids joyfully dancing with them. I was reminded of the reality that is parenting when my middle son, at first sight of a lightning bug, smashed it with his shoe and smeared it across the sidewalk. I pretty much knew then that there would be a learning curve to parenting.

Just when I thought parents had enough to worry about, I was reminded of more when I attended a conference about tech addiction. At its conclusion, I sat there full of anxiety. I was overcome with both positive and nervous energy. I was excited to share all I'd learned. But I was nervous because it reminded me of the important job we have as parents to curb technology to work for our kids, not against them, while maintaining our own healthy habits. The conference left me with a feeling of doomsday. But it was also hopeful. I left armed with statistics and confirmation that the things I feared about technology are backed by research and fact. Naturally, I took twenty pages of notes. Overall, it reminded me of a recurring theme. Doing our best as parents is important. Applied to technology, it means not overdoing it, filtering out the bad, and talking about it.

I love learning, so I signed up for another conference on a similar topic. It was a virtual one this time, which meant I would have a relaxing day of learning in the comfort of my home. I was looking forward to a chance to dive deep into a topic I feel so passionate about. Instead, it was a hectic day. The type of day that occurs so often in my life that I now welcome as a challenge. After I succeeded in getting tired, anxious kids ready for school, I found they were too sick to attend. So instead of my carefree work from home day, I got to balance it with sick kids. The worst of the challenge, though, was to not give in to the very thing that I was learning how to prevent: tech addiction in my children. As I stared at a screen in front of them for hours on end, I was convicted by research-based phrases like, "Don't be there physically but emotionally unavailable staring at a screen in front of them."

In addition to learner, teacher, and maker of lunches for sick children, I tasked myself with breaking the habit of allowing extended TV time when they are sick because the stats I was thrown are so alarming. During the online conference, I was shown visuals of the effects of technology on a developing brain, so I scrambled to find activities more entertaining than the screen. I spent much of the day feeling like a hypocrite, pacing around with headphones or staring at my laptop, holding on to hope that all the notetaking I was doing on actual paper was what they'd noticed. Overall, I found myself overwhelmed as a parent trying to do it right in this tech age. As an educator, I became overcome with the impact parenting has on student success. I know parental influence reaches far past the diploma. But despite the challenges of working in front of my children like many of us did during lockdown, the impact of the information was worth it. I became emotionally charged from the graphic case studies and alarming statistics, and extra motivated to work toward change. When I spend hours on a screen for work, I get physically drained. However, it is nothing compared to the repercussions of our children being drained by the screen. I was lucky enough to grow up before the screen and to have parents who gave me the freedom to do all the things that are now prescribed by pediatricians and listed as strategies to curb tech addiction.

We owe it to our children to bring things like outdoor play, free time, and boredom back to the forefront. So brace yourselves parents. A lot of the important work comes from us. We have the difficult task to create successful readers, physically active humans, non-polarizing community members, and overall good and healthy people.

One day my Apple newsfeed was flooded with articles paraphrasing a WSJ article, "Facebook knows Instagram is toxic for teen girls, company documents show"[1] I thought to myself, *Instagram is bad for teens, and it's official, so should we actually do something about that?* I read the lengthy article, thought about sharing it on my Facebook page, and almost wrote my own recap piece. But a sense of learned helplessness took over. I wondered, *Does it even make a difference to know what's bad for us, for each other, for the environment if we aren't even able to, or worse, willing to change our behavior?* Because knowing all of this bad stuff is just downright depressing if there's little movement toward improvement.

To start, it is noteworthy that the findings stated social media, or Instagram specifically, were not found to be harmful for all teens. There are many pros to the use of social media. Why was there a large study regarding Instagram-use specifically? One article stated that "on average, teens in the U.S. spend 50% more time on Instagram than they do on Facebook."[2] So it makes sense that they wanted to study one of the larger and more popular platforms that's been around for a while.

Focus groups, online surveys, diary studies, and large-scale surveys led to the "conclusion that some of the problems were specific to Instagram, and not social media more broadly. That is especially true concerning so-called social comparison, which is when people assess their own value in relation to the attractiveness, wealth and success of others."[3] In contrast to other teen-popular social media apps, like Tik-Tok and Snapchat, "Instagram focuses heavily on the body and lifestyle."[4] It elaborated with how Instagram users have "the tendency to share only the best moments, a pressure to look perfect and an addictive product can send teens spiraling toward eating disorders, an unhealthy sense of their own bodies and depression, March 2020 internal research states."[5]

The article also gets into the issue that Facebook, who owns Instagram, is knowingly deceiving the public. They compare their actions of not disclosing links between the apps usage and depression to that of Big Tobacco, who had kept the public in the dark about correlations between smoking and lung cancer.

Maybe I'm being pessimistic, but when we are told information that should be inspiring us to change, it sometimes comes across as something we don't really need to worry about. Something that will just work itself out. Or something that is just being exaggerated. Regarding this topic specifically, I sense that we all nod our heads and think, *Duh, of course Instagram is bad for teens.* It's nothing that we didn't already sort of know. Are we too overcome with all the things wrong in the world to even personally commit to applying the findings?

I'd feel more optimistic if other important research seemed to change our behaviors. We know smoking can cause lung cancer, and buying plastic straws causes harm to the oceans. But I wonder how far it goes to actually change our behavior. I admittedly used to read too many news articles, but I know there are others who have a constant vortex of worry swirling around their heads of all the problems of the world.

- Overconsumption of plastic

- Too little recycling

- Overproduction of clothing

- Poor animal conditions

- Too much exhaust air

- etc., etc., etc.

We may express worry about these things, but are we really doing all we can to change them? We know we shouldn't pack a family gathering full of plastic silverware, but it is just easier. I'm aware that much of my recycling doesn't end up recycled, so sometimes I mix it in with the trash. I try not to buy cheap clothing, but it is just so much . . . well, cheaper. I try and commit to pricier, free-range chicken, but does that even matter?

There's the research that we all knew existed in the back of heads that (shocker) there are some hefty consequences to social media use, especially in our youth. But are the words, "Instagram is bad for teens" just going to get half-ass commitment to change, or worse, sit by the wayside like so many others? How can we actually put some of this good research into use? The skeptic in me says that we will never be able to make real change in the virtual world. But I do feel it is one area that we do have personal control that can make a real difference. What can we do about the finding that Instagram is bad for teens, or bad for humanity in general? We can do a lot on a personal level. Because following what others are doing has never changed anything. We can stop using the platforms, or we can adjust their use based on our own comfort level. We can start by conducting a self-assessment to determine our level of discomfort with Instagram use, or that of our teens. Identifying if we or our children are negatively affected by Instagram use has to happen first. I don't have a teen yet; my children are too young to know Instagram exists (yay!). But when I observed in myself that Instagram wasn't serving my life, I conducted a personal experiment to see if I could coexist with social media in general.

Now that we know social media is unhealthy for us, should we keep on, hoping we "grow out of it"? When we find that Instagram is indeed bad for our mental state, what should we do? Should we quit Instagram? Make our children quit it? Ultimately, I think we should each find a balance that works. In discovering that Facebook and Instagram made me feel less than amazing, the action I took wasn't black and white. Some parts of the platforms are useful to me, and some just had to go. I can't control many of the problems of the world, but I found I could control this one in my personal life. The hope is that I can apply this same strategy to helping my children through it when they are teens.

Talking to our kids is important. As a high school educator, I've observed the discomfort that social media causes some our young people. Unfortunately, the digital age will always be a part of their world. Whether it's something they fight to refrain from, or something they choose not to live without, proper use of tech will be a challenge. In accepting that social media will always be around, we can work on creating a healthy relationship with it. Instagram alone is a wonderful place to display uniqueness and various forms of art. Even if it were to go away, it would quickly be replaced by something else. Unfortunately, our works of art, selfies, and words are readily on display to be validated or invalidated in a moment's time. Youth will continuously have to find the right way to coexist with social media, just as they will with any relationship in their life. Maybe the balance can be found in talking to therapists, reading self-help books, or talking to friends and family. In any case, talking about it is the first step in not allowing this problem to fall by the wayside.

In schools, we are in this weird time where educators don't yet feel comfortable dishing out advice about technology. The high school that I am a special educator at stopped allowing cell phones during class time starting in the 2023–2024 school year. Prior to that, it was appalling what could be seen in class and in the hallways between classes. As part of my position, I would frequently do observations of students in their classroom to observe on and off task behavior. It was common for 60 percent or more of their time to be spent staring at their phone. My write-ups of those observations looked like this: "Student was staring down at their lap. Student had AirPods in." Worse, we would spend almost every staff meeting discussing how we could limit students' cell phone use.

Districts spend thousands of dollars training us on best practices. I went to a tech addiction training, and I came back still feeling that it was not *allowable* for me to share the advice from respected researchers. I was even in a meeting where a dad flat-out asked us if he should limit his child's screen use, but no one elected to give their two cents. Many times, we have observed a correlation between a student's difficulties and their reported tech use, but we do not yet feel prepared to advise parents on how to manage it. Perhaps the reason it feels uncomfortable is that discussing technology use in a negative light is not yet common. It took several decades for it to become common and acceptable to tell someone who lights up a cigarette that they should perhaps quit. There is neither enough research nor enough discussion of the research on tech use, just yet.

I'm not going to pretend like I know what it's like to be a young person today. I am raising young people, and as a special education teacher, I have the opportunity to influence kids. Not in the post-2010-influencer sense, but in the live, flesh-and-bones sense. I was lucky to be in the generation that got to experience life without smartphones. It's why I yearn for young people today to live even an ounce of that life today. It's not that I think all technology is bad, but a lot of it can be.

As parents, we seem to be failing in letting kids be kids. We talk to them about their screens as if they are making the decision. Of course, they will choose the screen, just as they would choose a cupcake when it is an option for dinner. It is our job to create better boundaries, rules, and opportunities for discussions for them. We've made it acceptable for us to ignore our kids, and unacceptable for them to interrupt us. I wonder, would my parents have allowed endless iPad and screen pacifying? How could they not if they were given the option? Memories at my grandparents' home makes me think of lost opportunities for memory-making today when kids are appeased with a screen. Some of my best memories are from the creative ventures we had to come up with when we were bored at our grandparents' house. I tell stories of these days to my kids even today. I want the same for them. When my six-year-old gets hooked on games on my phone, I am mad at no one but myself. If I only could put my energy into one thing, it would be better tech habits in the home.

PROTECT SIMPLICITY:

- ***Give yourself grace.*** My three boys, ages ten and under, used to race down before eight a.m. to get to their beloved Xbox first. On good weeks, I remember to hide the controllers in a spot good enough they can't find. In honest moments, I admit to myself that the twenty-minute increments where they won and stole the controllers are nice. I admit I sometimes prefer when they have the controllers in hand and are whisked away to a land that doesn't involve asking me for cereal, or making a mess of their toys in the kitchen, or fort-making with my expensive couch in the living room. But these are the moments to look at the benefits of long-term discipline.

Give yourself grace, so that moments of weakness don't cause you to give up entirely.

- ***Make your kids communicate in words, in person.*** Communication skills will come at a premium in the future. One of the reasons my husband and I strive for less tech is that we want to put our kids in situations where they have to speak. We don't put them on screens when we go out to eat. We've had them ordering their own food *with eye contact* since they could talk. We know that good communication will be a marketable skill that will set those who have it above others when they are searching for a job, good friends, and a good partner in life.

- ***Do things as a family***. Make a list of some family activities. Mine are relatively simple. Enjoying a mug of calming tea while I watch them dance. (Being their biggest fan means the world to them.) They make sure I'm really watching too. Have dinner as a family, taking turns asking questions. Engage in an activity of their choice (sledding, nerf gun fight). Taking a drive with some tunes, or watching a movie/show of their choice.

- ***Write out a plan with your spouse.*** Map out a plan for when you want to introduce or allow various technologies. Discuss reasons for each decision so that you are prepared when your kids question them. My spouse and I discuss our stance on various aspects of technology until we come to an agreement. First, we want to be prepared for when the kids question why their friends have an allowance that they don't. For example, when they ask why they don't get their own tablet, smartphone, or unlimited video game play, we have a response ready. We can keep notes on the tech we do have and why. We can adequately explain that a smartphone is not needed for entertainment when they already have an Xbox. Next, we want to communicate a plan for when it would be appropriate and necessary for them to have, say a smartwatch, smartphone, or use of social media, for example. Finally, together we reinforce rules and strategies that go along with the technologies used at each stage of their lives. Having a plan helps you avoid the temptation to impulsively give in to what others are doing, or what your kids ask for, but instead stay true to your own judgement, decisions, and values.

- ***Show your kids empathy and model words when their friends question your tech rules.*** Explaining the whys to the kids. Giving them the words to use. Allow your kids a space to talk about how they feel about their friends having something they don't. Give them words they can respond with when their friends ask them why they don't have certain allowances. I tell my own kids to say things like, "The creators of smartphones also didn't let their kids have one." "My parents want me to practice using my imagination." "My parents don't like us overusing screens." My hope is that we will get to a point where low-tech devices are observed as desirable to younger generations. Where those sporting simple phones or watches won't have to explain themselves, but will instead be looked up to. Ask questions often. Don't assume you know how they are feeling. Ask your children questions about how they feel about your technology rules. Have discussions where you welcome their insight and opinions. Ask them about how their peers are interacting with technology. Ask them how they feel about their peers' various ways of interacting online.

- ***Transform observations into teachable moments.*** I now hear my child talk judgingly about poor tech behaviors, and I couldn't be prouder. He's smart, so he knows our new standards are seen as odd and not ideal, but I can see his wheels turning, wondering if he should conform or follow my guidance. He for sure will have to make those decisions to do what his friends are doing or to follow his own path once he's grown. In the little time I have to influence him, I am committed to modeling what it looks like to *unfollow.*

- ***Delay, delay, delay smartphones.*** In moments of weakness where I think about giving in to providing my children with a smartphone, the word "research" brings me back to reality. One of the reasons many parents give in is because we fear they will miss out or be outcast. Many parents may believe they are getting them as a safety and communication device. However, if that were the case, a "dumb phone" or watch would do. I admit I buy my children expensive shoes to fit in. However, I don't want to do so with a smartphone. Pricey shoes don't have negative repercussions of altered attention spans, physical posture, poor mental health. Designer shoes aren't being called the new cigarette. Getting them a smartphone before it is age appropriate because everyone else has one is not a good enough reason. Another reason I believe good-intentioned parents give in, is to avoid conflict. They really, really want one and we don't want to argue with our children. Unfortunately, conflict will always be there. It's about consciously choosing the right conflict. I am consciously choosing that our conflicts be over our stance versus their desire for a smartphone. I believe the alternative is what I observe at the high school with students attached to their phones. Conflicts over putting the smartphone away, limiting their smartphone time, moodiness related to misinterpreted conversations, and lack of engagement outside of it. Once we gift our child a phone, it becomes their most prized personal property. Fights will be over attempting to take "their" property. They will bring it everywhere, because that is what society has modeled as being done with a smartphone. Giving in too soon is gifting them a lifetime of smartphone habits. I've only had mine since adulthood began and can't imagine what a lifetime with it would do. At the very least, my desire is to delay the amount of time their lives are spent attached to the shiny box.

Chapter 18

Unfollow Wasting Precious Time

Your time is limited, so don't waste it following someone else's life.

As I began writing this chapter, I needed my iPhone handy to refer to the hundreds of iNotes I'd recorded on it. I observed myself getting distracted by a constant need to share a thought with someone via text message. Though I scheduled myself thirty measly minutes of uninterrupted writing time, I couldn't do the uninterrupted part with the phone in my hand. When a thought popped into my head of something I needed to communicate with someone, the fear that I would lose the thought forced me to send the message. In picking up the smartphone, it was game over. It led me to automatically check and respond to other text messages, which more often than not required me to check the family calendar and other sports apps. At that point, the individual I had texted had responded, which warranted another response from me.

If my phone is in sight, I have apps that I check on autopilot. I may sit down to write or do anything else, but the phone and the habit I've created wins the battle for my attention nearly every time. I no longer have the Facebook app, but I have Reddit, and when I'm having a sharp-brain day I stop myself and ask why I'm on Reddit when I know I have only allowed myself to keep that app for camaraderie with others in the evening. Before I know it, my thirty minutes have passed, and my productivity is gone by the wayside.

I like to sing the number of emails to the tune of the popular tune from Rent. "Five hundred, twenty-five thousand, six hundred emails!" It makes me laugh at the situation, so I don't cry. I had to make the decision at work to not check my email until the end of the day. If I respond too quickly, recipients will come to expect that, whether its nine p.m. on a Monday or nine a.m. on a Sunday.

I keep thinking about how emails and texts are always someone else's agenda. Instead of stopping what I am doing to complete someone else's to-do list, I want to focus on what I had set out to do. There's this battle for our attention. Even before screens were part of our daily life, our attention was divided. Worse now, not only is our attention divided between the screen and "real life," but our attention is divided between various avenues on the screen. Our attention easily drifts elsewhere when a notification arrives. Not only do we divide our attention between what we are doing online and what we are doing in person, but we also split it among the various tasks we perform on a screen. This constant multitasking wreaks havoc on our attention span. At first, I thought it was fine to keep Reddit on my smartphone. The app lets me dive into topics of my choice, allowing me to nurture my love of learning. However, I soon found myself opening the app dozens of times a day. I would scroll through Reddit before bed each night and couldn't put it down for at least an hour. I realized my attention span was suffering when I hadn't picked up a book or even tried watching a new show in weeks.

I've proven to myself time and time again that if I click on a social media app, I'm scrolling. Before I know it, whatever other task I had set out to do in that moment is gone. An entire afternoon could end with only having spent it viewing what others are doing or thinking. We only have so much time and energy. If we are putting that energy into texting, showing off our excursions online, and checking on other people, we leave little time and energy for actually living and engaging in real-life interactions.

PROTECT SIMPLICITY:

- ***Put notes on paper instead of on your smartphone***. The use of iNotes was a crutch I leaned on due to the distrust of my memory. However, intentional use of technology means cutting out excess ways that keep me staring at my screen. A simple replacement is having a small notebook with me. This helps keep the focus to utilizing the notes instead of doing that along with anything else the phone may pull you into. To prevent the screen from being a productivity killer, most of what I do is offline, then anytime left can go online.

- ***Use technology to delegate your time.*** Use of a digital calendar, echo, or alarms on your phone can help keep you on track instead of being guided, or derailed, by notifications. Having these accessible to the whole family keeps everyone in the know. Instead of the kids asking me what time their practice is, they can refer to the calendar. Instead of giving the kids a ten-minute warning before leaving, that can be announced on the Amazon Echo.

- ***Only check work-related messages at specific times***. I found that when I was checking work email all day, I would inadvertently prioritize whatever was sent. Early on in my teaching career, when I didn't know better than to not check work email at home, the stress from some emails could make me lose sleep. I count messages or tasks that have to be processed for the family or health as work too. Children's sports teams' apps, fitness and nutrition tracking, and medical appointments require the checking of apps, text messages, and email. They are important tasks that need to be completed. Setting a time and place can allow you to get the tasks done without derailing you from what you set out to do that day.

- ***Put your phone in a drawer when it is "productivity" time.*** I found this to be a huge step in my productivity. Hiding the phone from sight is an important piece to avoiding the compulsion to pick it up. No phone in view until the work is done.

- ***Have Facebook Events sent to your email.*** By doing this, you won't need to check Facebook and get lured into checking out the latest posts. I also turned off email notifications for any other Facebook mention, as before I did this, I was getting dozens of emails about someone posting something.

- ***Set a timer when going on a platform to look through someone's photos.*** When and if I find a good time to look through someone's virtual photo album, setting a timer is essential. An even better practice is to schedule time to see the person and look through the photos with them.

- ***Do not answer texts immediately.*** Unfortunately, text messages have morphed into email inboxes. We used to only get messages from family and friends. Businesses have discovered messaging is the quickest way to grab our attention. Email and app notifications are not enough. We now receive text messages for appointment reminders, questionnaires, and promotions. Answering texts immediately is prioritizing someone else's time over your own. Have set hours of the day to check in and respond. I also stopped apologizing when I didn't get back right away.

Chapter 19

Unfollow Digital Clutter

It's not how much we have, but how much we enjoy, that makes happiness.

—Charles Spurgeon

Bloggers like to collaborate with each other. A fellow blogger asked me to write a piece that she could share on her site. I told her I would write about applying popular decluttering strategies to the digital world. The last time I procrastinated in completing a writing task, it was a statistics report for a psychological study in college. I procrastinated the act of decluttering my digital space so much that I completely stopped writing for a year and a half. That essay was next on my list, so until I could write it, I wouldn't let myself write anything else, and I couldn't write it until I actually did the work of decluttering.

I'm still in that process of decluttering. Though my smartphone and laptop are not yet the crisp, clean minimalistic space I had envisioned, I did get back to writing. I just worked on the other parts of my mission to develop better tech habits first. I maintained consistency in my procrastination by making this one of the last stressors for me to tackle. I did learn something in the process. I learned that I could find acceptance in chaos as I take baby steps to declutter and develop techniques to prevent it in the first place.

Why is the process of digital decluttering such a hassle? The problem is multifaceted. The most pressing issue is that the clutter is already there, and space is limited. The clutter is spread out everywhere we roam in virtual space. Photos in the cloud take up space on my Google account that is shared with Gmail and Google Drive. I know this because I get frequent emails reminding me that my Google storage is full. Oh, and I also get emails reminding me of the $2.99 I spend each month to store it all. The photos on my iPhone are divided into shared albums, and iPhone created albums and collages too. There are photos and videos, and tagged photos and videos, on various social media platforms. So the first part is figuring out what to do with all of the photos, videos, documents, and large files in emails, and files on the desktop. Then, once you figure out how you want to open up storage on the Google account, and how you want to store photos, the second part is figuring out how to spend all of that time on the screen to do so. Taking too many photos not only robs our future self of time, but it forces us to make tedious and often difficult decisions. When my past self-decided to take ten photos of the same thing, it left me with the burden to delete a piece of a memory. Worse is that the thousands of photos stored in various places are hard to enjoy in this fashion. I've decided it's best to work slowly through the organization of digital clutter and put my energy into better habits that keep me from adding to the mess. I don't want to find myself with the same problem ten years from now.

PROTECT SIMPLICITY:

- ***Apply your favorite physical decluttering strategies to your digital space.*** Two of my favorite strategies come from *The Minimalists Podcast:*

  A packing party: The idea is to pretend you are moving and to pack up all of your belongings. Then, only take out of the boxes what you need to use. After some time, anything left goes away. Applied to digital space, I can pretend I have a new phone. In having a new phone, I can remove apps. Any apps I need I can add back. For added challenge, I can move all data (files, iNotes, photos) to a hard drive, which serve the same purpose as a box. This can also be done on a smaller scale, by going space by space (emails one day, photos another, smartphone home page, etc.).

The 30-day game: Here you remove as many items from your household as that day of the month. On day one you remove one item. Fast-forward to day thirty, and you remove thirty items. Applied to my digital space, I like to increase the amount by starting with the removal of, say, one hundred photos or emails each day. I write a tally mark for each day so I can see my progress.

Another strategy I use for both my physical and digital space is a mindset I came up with when it was difficult to toss something. I pretend that I never obtained the item. It was never gifted to me, and I never purchased it. Applied to my digital space, I might pretend I never took the photo. It helps me feel less guilty about removing or deleting something.

- ***Copy and paste information to print instead of screenshotting.*** Likely due to an increasingly shortened attention span, I often find articles I would like to read but have no willpower to read right then and there. I greatly distrust my memory. Therefore, I screenshot anything I want to refer back to. It is as if I am using screenshotting as an extension to my brain. At its highest count, I had a screenshot album of six thousand five hundred fifteen.

Copy and pasting information and sending it via email allows me the option to print. If I have a printed copy of something, I am more likely to read it.

- ***Be considerate of your future self.*** Anything you choose to add or keep is something your future self will eventually have to declutter. Every email I don't delete after reading and every photo I take is something my future self must address. Limit what you bring in from the start. Only allow things in if they have a clear purpose or place. For example, I limit the number of photos I take at each event, keeping in mind how I plan to use them. This mindset brings back the joy in photography. Applied to apps, it means being intentional about which ones you download, what features you add, and who or what you follow on social media. Placing limits on quantity helps you focus on quality.

- ***Store videos on hard drives.*** It's a tedious process, but removing videos from my iCloud frees up a lot of space. Using a hard drive also allows you to display videos or photos in formats beyond your smartphone. Watching home videos on television creates a better bonding experience than viewing them on individual screens.

- ***Share photos in real time***. If I waited to share photos until I had completed photo albums they would never be shared. Sending them right away to a digital frame or private Instagram account prevents procrastination from setting in. It's especially important to me for my kids to see the photos I take of them. After all, what is the point of posting photos of my kids to others if they don't get to share in on the memories themselves?

- ***Unsubscribe from email lists that no longer benefit you***. Most email providers now make unsubscribing simple. To opt out of text message subscriptions, you can usually reply with "STOP." Consider setting aside a couple of hours to eliminate unwanted notifications. Similarly, be mindful about sharing your phone number or email just to receive a "deal." If you do, unsubscribe right after your purchase.

- ***Regularly reevaluate your collection of apps, contacts, friends, followers, etc.*** Nothing invasive is worth your peace of mind. If you download an app, it does not mean it needs to stay on your device forever. What may have been useful years ago, or even days ago, may not be needed now, so it's important to regularly determine if something still provides value. If it no longer does, then let it go.

Chapter 20

Unfollow Family Disruptions

People first, and then things.

—Joshua Fields Milburn

I was deep into reading at the public library when a lady shouted across the room to the librarian. This interrupted my calm and also threw me off guard. We are taught and trained from a young age to be quiet in a library. I realized I wanted my home to mimic a library. Not in the sense that it is quiet, but that it has its own social code. I want my home to be happy and safe with moments of calm (as enduring calm is not attainable). I want a home that is not silent like a library, and not loud and overstimulating like a dance club, but somewhere in the middle. So I set out to create it. My husband and I go back and forth on whether we should put an addition onto our three-bedroom ranch home. We are conflicted because we don't truly need the space. We like to be around each other. Without one-to-one devices, we are close to each other a lot, and we do okay with that. It also forces us outside more. I want a healthy balance that's somewhere between the "quiet as a mouse" home I've seen and the chaotic, nonstop action home I grew up in and experience today. The quiet end of the culture I observe is one where children are scheduled at most hours of the day and then "rewarded" for their hard work with screen time. They spend most of their day being told what to do. They then come home and, instead of sharing with their family, they tune out on the screen.

There are eerily quiet homes where everyone is in their own corner, hypnotized by a screen. There are large homes with much space left unused. Some homes are full of people who have become uncomfortable experiencing downtime. I wonder why so much physical space is actually needed if they are plugged into their own world, or not even home enough to enjoy the space. Our home hovers more on the chaotic end. The boys argue a lot, and though my husband and I both have the summer off from teaching, we have our small business, amongst the other new activities that come with summer.

There is a short window of time when the summer break with a young family is enjoyable. There is a window of time we are elated the school responsibilities have subsided. After that initial weekend, though, it hits us. If we are not ready with clear boundaries and routines, chaos ensues. Adding a video game console to our family dynamic added to the chaotic nature. It created quite the open sore for me. I once heard that the toughest ages to parent are eight through ten. This made me feel better because it *has* been tough. Attempting to find balance with a preferred activity (the Xbox) has made it all the more challenging.

It's not that my kids don't play outside or that they are on tech-addict level (though debatable for my youngest), but the gaming console does cause a lot of tension in our home and has wreaked havoc on our family dynamic. When it came to video games, the boys fought us when it was time to put it away. They threw things when they lost. My youngest once told me he loves the Xbox more than me. (He was joking, of course, but I sensed some truth in what he said.) My spouse and I disagreed on the subject. He felt they should play because it's a normal thing for kids to do, which I agreed with—to an extent. I'd take it away, but as has occurred in other parts of my parenthood life, then ultimately give in later for fear they'd be left out of what their friends were doing. The other part of our family dynamic that added to the chaos was this game where my kids asked for things, usually tech-related, and we said no. I hated feeling like I was mean mom. We half-heartedly tried different approaches until we got serious about preserving the calm(ish) and happy home we wanted.

To create a happy home, we need to raise kind, responsible individuals. The most important thing to me is protecting and nurturing the family unit, which means building a foundation of trust and support within our home. Our goal is to foster a family environment where everyone genuinely enjoys spending time together, even after the children have grown and left home. We strive to raise emotionally healthy children who become productive members of society. Through our actions and the rules my spouse and I set, we want our children to know that we truly value spending quality time as a family.

PROTECT SIMPLICITY:

- ***Have whole family rules.*** Family dynamics are strengthened when rules are applied to all members, including parents. Ideas like "screen breaks" or rules like "we exercise our brains and our bodies before screen use" are easy to understand. Saying them often and consistently following them in front of them encourages buy-in from children. Rules like "no screens at meals" are easy for everyone to follow. With active children, we have limited situations where we can talk. Meal time is one of those. Uninterrupted meal time is a good time to practice a sense of community, not to mention language development. In creating and following rules with our children we teach them collaboration, communication, and problem-solving skills that will serve them throughout their lives.

- ***Disallow bullying or bad sportsmanship at home.*** Use video games as a tool to instill the same sportsmanship standards as coaches do on their sports teams. Video game play is competitive. A certain amount of arguing is normal with siblings. However, I want video games to serve a purpose if I am going to allow them. Therefore, when the kids fight while playing them, I like to use these times as teachable moments. I'd most certainly not allow them to play baseball if at every game they chucked the bat across the field. So I ask them if that behavior would be allowable in, say, a baseball game. Then we discuss better ways to interact that would be allowable in a real-life game.

- ***Let go of fears that keep you from limiting screen time.*** I often have to curb the fear that I will not be able to relax unless I provide a screen to my child. In addition, I am sometimes driven by the fear that if we disallow video games at too many playdates, we will be known as the "boring house." But these are just stories my fear tells me. There is no way our home isn't fun. Giving in for that reason is like the households who supply alcohol under the guise of safety or to be the "cool" parents. Perhaps it's better to show kids that a life with less alcohol is more favorable too. Along the same lines, trust that your child can be sent to a sleepover without a device. There is nothing bad that can come from kids using their imaginations more. I even join in on their imagination play, as it is good for adults too.

- ***Ignore others' fears being projected on you.*** We live in a small town, in between the middle of the shops and schools. Therefore, a lot of people we know often drive by. What I love is when people tell us how wonderful it is to see us outside all the time. However, as is life, there will always be differing opinions. A neighbor often texted me, worried about our kids' bike riding, or basically just existing outside, often sarcastically calling my parenting style "free range." Her reprimand almost made me want to keep them contained and plugged in like she did with her kids. But then I remembered that she is adding to an anxious generation that I want no part of. I realized I was in control of what messages I allowed to infiltrate my day. There was no rule that says once you add someone to your phone contact list you must keep them. Therefore, I utilized the blocking feature so we could continue to live out our own values.

- ***Make the use of screens a privilege instead of something you give in to.*** There are great moments of peace when the kids are on video games or smartphones. But much like there are great moments of peace when we treat them to ice cream, there are repercussions. The sugar rush is similar to the tech brain, aka overstimulation brain. It is best to pick special times when their other basic needs are met so I know that they can handle the overstimulation.

- ***Reinforce a culture of support.*** With three boys, there is a healthy amount of competition between them. However, I wanted to make sure I was helping them cheer each other on too. I encourage them to be happy for each other during sporting events, when they talk about the fun they had on their playdate, and even when they won the game on the Xbox. I am working on using the technology devices we do have as tools for supporting each other's ambitions. Since our smartphones sit in a designated home, and the children don't have their own, I explicitly teach them how to use the features that support them. Don't assume they know how to make a phone call, send a text, or write an email. I avoid calling it "my phone" but intentionally make it a family device. This reinforces them to utilize it in productive ways, such as independently, and appropriately communicating with others.

- ***Repeat procedures and language often.*** My child called me out one day for instantly responding to a text as we were busy doing something else. He said to me, "Talk about tech addiction." I couldn't be prouder of him, and I made sure to correct my behavior. I leave a list of "digital vegetables" out that they can use at any time (learning and music apps), as well as non-tech activities (crafts, instruments, sports equipment, etc.). Repeating phrases like "digital vegetables" or "screen breaks" helps the entire family to ease into routines.

Chapter 21

Commitment to Continuous Experimentation

Don't be too timid and squeamish about your actions. All life is an experiment. The more experiments you make the better.

—Ralph Waldo Emerson

My first experiment regarding intentionality with technology was back in 2020. It had a title and everything: "Does This Online Tool Bring Me Joy? A Personal Experiment with Social Media Hypothesis." I can be happy in the virtual world if I clear out the social media clutter and keep only those parts that add value to my life.

Steps to Evaluate Digital Necessity:

- Take a break from any social media platform that's bothering you. (For example, I stopped using Facebook and Instagram.)

- Make a list of both real-life activities and social media activities using some variation of The Pleasure-Predicting Method (described below).

- Record observations of time spent on these activities and how much joy was actually felt.

- Commit to spending the majority of your time on those things that bring you the most joy.

- Adjust your social media accounts by deleting them or changing them to only include parts that add value or joy to your life.

Years ago, I was lucky enough to come across a reading from psychologist David D. Burns, where he offered a slew of methods for living your best life. Some of his research is on cognitive distortions and the strategies for untwisting your thinking. The Pleasure-Predicting Method is one of those strategies that can be used to combat procrastination or prove to ourselves that we don't need others to feel satisfied in our life. For the sake of this experiment, I used it to identify activities (mostly offline, but some online) that bring me joy. First, Burns asks us to list an activity—who it will be with; can be oneself— and what percentage we predict our satisfaction will be. Then, after spending time on the activities, the percentage of satisfaction we actually felt is recorded.[1] I decided that any activity that brought me less than 50 percent enjoyment, I would spend 50 percent or less of my time on it.

In order to assure I am spending most of my time on activities that bring me joy, I made that recommended list. In order to live out social media minimalism, or even digital minimalism, it means included activities that are both online and in person. Some parts of social media bring me joy, but I had a hard time enjoying them without clearing out the social media clutter. Below is the list of activities from that moment in my life and my predicted enjoyment for each of them. It contains both real-life and virtual activities in no particular order.

- Playing games with my kids: 90%

- Writing: 85%

- Blogging: 85%

- Recording music: 70%

- Using Facebook Messenger: 60%

- Texting friends and family: 95%

- Snapchatting select friends and family: 80%

- Running: 85%

- Doing CrossFit: 90%

- Watching Netflix: 85%

- Sketching/Painting: 60%

- Reading specific Apple News articles: 80%

- Posting on Instagram or Facebook: 45%

- Scrolling through Facebook or Instagram newsfeeds: 5%

- Checking Facebook or Instagram notifications: 25%

- Hanging out with friends in small or individual groups: 90%

- Date night: 75%

- Family activities with the husband and kids: 95%

- Virtual get-togethers (FaceTime chat): 60%

- Conducting and writing about a social media experiment: 85%

Right away, I realized something. Those things we spend our time on that do nothing for us mimic one-sided relationships that leave us feeling drained. Filtering out these activities opens the door for the important things we are meant to do. In observing my life with less and more individualized presence online, I had many revelations. Taking time to reflect led me to success in finding a relationship with various platforms that work for me. Losing my smartphone for almost a week made me realize how much this little device ruled my world. After the expected day in stress mode, I immediately started reaping the benefit of this "loss." Since I was a pursuer of digital minimalism, I knew the universe was giving me that last push I needed. Days after posting a sarcastic poem of my love-hate relationship with my phone, it seemed to take revenge. On the Friday night of a busy gym event, I frantically stashed my iPhone in my sweatpants as I got myself, the kids, and the house ready. The first hint from the universe came through in a thought: *I'm afraid of losing my phone, so I'm keeping it in the tiny pocket of my sweatpants.*

I packed up the car, the babysitter arrived, and I left. The car's Bluetooth connection signaled that I didn't have my phone with me, so I left knowing it was at home. Fast-forward to midnight and ten inches of snow, and I went out to shovel the driveway. When I got back inside, I realized my phone was lost. I searched the house, gave up, and went to bed. The next five days were spent searching through piles of snow and every room in the house. I refused to buy a new one. It helped when Monday arrived and I remembered the iPad I had stashed away, giving me access to texting and some apps. By day six, I felt changed. Yes, I bought a new phone, but I gave myself a rule: I wasn't allowed to activate it until I typed up what I had learned. This is when I felt that the universe was on my side. I typed up my lesson learned and activated the new phone—then found my old phone two minutes later (in one of two snow piles I had yet to get to).

I thank the universe for the laugh and for these lessons:

1. My fixation on my phone was getting out of control. I fixated on my phone when it was lost as much as I did when I had it.

This was the most alarming thing I learned about my phone usage. For the first two days, my kids watched me relentlessly clean out every square inch of the house—from garage to basement— muttering that I couldn't believe I had lost my phone. I even went so far as to kick through every pile of snow in our yard.

Every time they walked by me, they asked, "Have you found your phone yet, Mom?" I probably uttered the word cell phone two hundred times that first forty-eight hours. They definitely left the weekend feeling like Mom's cell phone really meant a lot to her. I sulked in that realization, then decided that while I wouldn't halt my search and rescue mission, I would make it less obvious and give it less attention. I am grateful for the reminder not to fixate on my phone when with my loved ones. They deserve better.

2. *I thrive when I don't have social media at my fingertips.* Losing my smartphone helped me decipher between what I valued for connection purposes (texting, and Snapchat) and what I liked using for information and communication (checking events, invites, and pages on Facebook; reading and sharing bursts of info and videos on Instagram). It also reinforced which apps were best to have on my phone versus those I should just access on my laptop as needed.

*3. **I don't have a phone addiction, but I was getting close.***
Smartphone addiction is not an actual disorder yet. But I found an article titled "6 behavioral criteria that had the highest diagnostic accuracy for the diagnosis of smartphone addiction" that said the main criteria for evaluation was "heightened attention to using or quitting smartphone use."[2] I know that I could not ever have given my phone away purposefully for six days. Looking back, I can't believe I ever brought it to Mass, took it out at a restaurant, or stared at it when talking to my sons. In addition, the article identified four functional criteria, with "use in a physically hazardous situations (such as while driving or crossing the street) or situations that have other negative impacts on daily life."[3] That was alarming to me. I found that when I was driving around those couple of days without a phone, I felt *bored*. My normal behavior being to turn to my phone during red lights or bad songs. I often tell my kids, "I can't *do* anything else. The thing I'm doing is driving" when they ask me to do things while driving. I realized that I may not always practice what I preach when I am driving alone.

4. ***My life is too hectic.*** I am 0 percent surprised that I lost my phone on a Friday with all that I had to get done in order to get out the door. I need to take some things off my plate.

5. ***I have been letting my brain turn to mush.*** When I drove places I'd been to a dozen times, I got incredibly lost. I barely knew how to read a paper map. (Impressively, we did have one!) I didn't know what to do with my time when I didn't have a phone to tinker with. I forgot how to use my imagination on the road or to fall asleep. Reading was too slow; even full-length movies felt too long in comparison to short bursts of reels. There have got to be major repercussions coming from the short attention spans being created today.

6. ***I want to optimize communicating with those I love.*** At first the world just stopped. I instantly felt isolated. I also felt stressed about all those who would be trying to get ahold of me. Once I had reactivated my iPad and was able to reply to text messages, I felt better and gained clarity. Many of the conversations I worried about missing would happen one way or another. That's because those who really needed to talk to me would find me. And if they didn't, it wasn't important. Did I need to be checking work and personal email every five minutes? No! It felt good to talk to my kids or my husband without simultaneously looking down at my phone.

7. ***I need to not put all my eggs in one basket.*** I instantly worried about losing the thousands of iNotes I have on my smartphone. The irony is that so many ideas get stuck in the world of

iNotes, never to be shared with anyone, and only to be at risk of being lost (if not saved to the cloud). Losing my phone jumpstarted me out of writers' block, reintroduced me to writing on paper, and reminded me to think less and share more.

8. ***My phone (and home) was more cluttered than I thought.*** Seeing the old apps on the iPad that I haven't used since 2021 made me think about how I tend to keep every app I've ever installed. Really, these should come and go as I change. It provided clarity into what apps add value to my life and made deleting those that don't fairly easy. Along the same lines, when I turned the house upside down for a week, I learned all the hidden spots clutter was hanging out.

9. ***Keeping a smartphone lying around makes being present almost impossible.*** Overall, I loved being without my phone. When it's near me, the compulsion to check it is so robotic its comical. A message is rarely an emergency, and usually someone else's agenda to fulfill. Notifications usually require me to stop what I'm doing and act. Without all the pings, a weight lifted off my shoulders. I didn't have to risk losing my attention, calmness, or focus. I enjoyed the forced peacefulness so much that I dreaded having one with me 24/7 again. Though

I'll keep a smartphone around, I know that it serves me well to give it a home for most of the day.

10. ***Self-experimentation with the digital world is important and never a closed case***. At first, I was unsure how I truly felt about the ability to simply give up certain technologies. Hearing messages that say "technology is bad" made me want to give it up entirely. But this forced experiment made me trust that it can be a tool instead of a hindrance if I continue to pay attention to the signs. Overall, we must commit to figuring out what works for us individually. Even when we find useful strategies, we have to adapt them to work for us. As a special educator at the high school level, a lot of what I teach students with disabilities are organizational skills. (Think student with ADHD and what deficits they need to be taught.) I used to teach the same organizational skills. We were given a school-issued planner, so I required students to write in it. It was a small notebook with motivational quotes, academic formulas, and grammar rules and had lined pages to write one's assignments on. After 90 percent of my students failed to comply, along with my attempt to utilize this system as well, I observed how my own organization changes from time to time (sometimes as often as week to week).

I brainstormed other methods they could try: recording memos in the phone, using different binders or notepads for each subject (or in my case, life category), putting tasks in a virtual calendar so they can get the feeling of accomplishment after they mark it "accomplished." But I mainly encouraged them to self-reflect. I personally bought into the pretty spiral notepads meant to assist you with keeping your life in order. I wrote a dozen sticky notes a day and lost 50 percent of them by noon. I now use the notebook system in combination with an online calendar. I've tried implementing organizational journals (be it travel, self-help, cooking, etc.), none of which have worked for me. As the social media age came, I tried to follow methods that people claimed were life-changing. I took notes, screen-shot, and followed pages that seemed like they had that one thing I needed to make some aspect of my life easier.

We are human, so the strategies that work today may not next week. We can't just blindly follow one method that worked for one person. Throughout our lives, we will be told about that *one* idea, that *one* strategy, or that *one* app that will make all the difference in your life. I geeked out over *Atomic Habits* by James Clear and adopted the pieces that work for me. I love the strategies in the book *The 5 AM Club* by Robin Sharma. But my version of it is starting my day at six a.m. I begin my day doing CrossFit with an amazing group at six a.m., a task I avoided for twelve years and one I will surely keep forever, God willing. Yet if I put off working out in the morning because I wasn't making that five a.m. time, convincing myself I was a failure because I wasn't following that author's formula to a T, then I never would've found myself in the ideal place for me in this current day and time. We have to trust ourselves to know what's right.

But what truly helped me succeed was something I realized I had innately done long ago. I observed myself by analyzing what worked for me from the strategies I had instinctively tried, or ones I had been taught, and I followed the beat of my own drum. It feels like just yesterday when I was senior in high school and I started the habit of writing and rewriting the definitions of psychology vocabulary for an upcoming test. I did this throughout college as well. Fast-forward to adulthood (true adulthood, like mortgage, kids, and responsibilities) and I had lost confidence in discovering what worked for me. Distracted by temptations from others via all the apps, I was influenced to believe the answer to my current disorganized life was online.

Upon going online, I noticed the advertising was so good. I felt these strangers posed as professionals had all the answers. I felt that if I landed on the right phrase, video, strategy, or book, then all my problems would be solved. I had to go through the lesson of wasting my (and my students') time to learn that what works best is to take the advice and the tools and make them work for me individually. To not take them wholly, but to take bits and pieces and put it together in my own way.

Chapter 22

The Digital World Is Unavoidable; Intentionality Is Key

It's not good enough to say, I'm gonna stop watching this stuff, I'm gonna stop consuming this stuff, you've gotta ask what am I gonna start doing instead in order to get that adventure in a way that's healthy.

—T.K. Coleman

Living intentionally in a digital age doesn't automatically mean having zero social media accounts, a "dumb phone," and zero televisions. In fact, I find that the use of a smartphone and social media are somewhat of a necessity in my own life. I also know that in opening the can of worms that is those things, I can be tempted to overuse them as an escape—from discomfort or from life in general. Living with intention, simply put, it is the allowance of what is valuable into our lives.

In order to focus on the value a smartphone, social media, and even "digital candy" (such as a video game) can provide, creating rules, habits, and practices that filter out the good and leave out the bad can become tools that enhance instead of wreak havoc. Maintaining set rules and procedures is an easy way to keep the peace in a household. Instead of tech use being at the will of parents, children can utilize various technologies as tools at will. Less combative than saying no to screen use, redirecting to non-tech or better tech activities, or yanking screens from young people is having rules and procedures to refer to. Applying rules to tangible items like smartphones, video game consoles, and tablets are slightly easier to be intentional with. Fighting the temptation to go against personal values, or to interrupt life to engage in social media, can be a bit more complicated.

So where am I in the process today? Identifying which social media platforms to utilize and how to use them is like finding a perfect sleep number on a Sleep Number bed. Just because I can't find my perfect sleep number doesn't mean I shouldn't sleep; it just means I should keep trying until I find it. When it comes to social media, it's no secret that I dislike many things about it. But in my search for intentionality of all things, I did find some value in engaging online for these particular reasons.

- Promoting our small business, my writing, and my band

- Learning and personal growth

- Sharing with others

- Connecting with a small group of loved ones

These reasons make some parts of social media valuable to me personally. I do, however, refuse to succumb to simply *being* on social media. You'll notice that these reasons for being on social media were not listed above:

- So people know I exist

- So people know what my kids look like and are doing regularly

- To regularly share altered/filtered photos of myself

- So I can like others' photos to demonstrate that I care for them

- To escape reality

Instead, I focus my energy on being very intentional with my social media usage. I don't blindly use the various platforms like I did before. I have neither the time nor the mental capacity to do so. I now use each social media account for specific purposes. Here's how I work to be intentional with technology use in the various ways I deem it beneficial to my own life.

How I Am Intentional with Social Media Use as a Writer

1. ***Collaborating with others in the same field of interest:*** Just when I was going to go at writing alone, I realized the value in the online community. Following and engaging with various topics on blogs, or even on Reddit, in similar interest areas as mine is supportive in a good way. I feel as though I can't expect others to value my words if I don't value the words of others. It's fun to problem-solve with others in new ventures and engage in conversation about our commonalities.

2. ***Posting less frequently, but more thoughtfully to public accounts:*** Much to my dismay, being a blogger and aspiring author requires some usage of social media. If I want others to read my words, I have to meet them where they are. In keeping some social media platforms for the sake of sharing my message, I have to be careful not to let bad habits take away from my real life. I carefully choose platforms that allow me to get more bang for my buck. I use the public accounts to share articles I've written. I unfollow others so I can limit distractions and keep up with others' lives on my terms. I intentionally keep people on my account and add others to increase my reach. I don't limit others from sharing photos of me, or tagging me in photos, as that allows others to see how I

am living out my own message. Having an account where I post a powerful photo from time to time helps demonstrate the message I am working to convey: ***You can follow your own rules online.*** I want those who see my account to see a person who is not often online but is still thriving. In sharing personal photos with loved ones privately, I focus my energy on intentionally posting for the sharing of my message.

How I Am Intentional with Social Media Use for Promotional Purposes

Maintaining an online presence for our small business has challenged me to be intentional with social media use. My husband and I weren't about to work hard on a second career for more than a decade, only to ignore the benefits of using social media to support it. I can't speak for him, but here is how I am intentional with my social media use in terms of helping it maintain its online presence.

1. ***Outsourcing tasks:*** In the beginning, I gave advertising a go. He then gave it a go and was definitely better at multitasking, utilizing templates and scheduling apps. More than ten years in, we now use creative ways (bartering) to have those who are content in making content, to do it for us. At this point, we

do not put any focus into engagement with other pages or individuals; we find just getting regular content on our page out there is enough. This outsourcing allows us to focus our energy on big-picture items related to the business. If we find we can no longer afford to barter or pay someone to do content creation, our plan is to go back to scheduling posts.

2. ***Adding to our sense of community:*** As a fitness center, we find Facebook useful for adding to our sense of community. As much as we want to live social media-free, our business has its own identity. If people are online, it's important we meet them there. As 90 percent of our members use Facebook, we maintain a private page to communicate community events and share humor and wins. We do, however, prioritize the creation of real-life opportunities for social engagement.

How I Am Intentional with Social Media Use as a Lifelong Learner

1. ***Using specific platforms to work toward my goals:*** With a busy real life, there is literally a finite amount of time I am able to deem "me time." Like I mentioned earlier, I simply tidied up this me time that used to be filled with mindless scrolling. Now I read articles specifically in the areas in my life I am looking to improve. There is value in reading others' stories. I mostly read books, but I occasionally allocate this

time to blogs, or even social media pages. If I didn't believe that some content provides value, I wouldn't share any content at all myself. To keep in line with intentionality, I utilize various platforms that help me solve problems or make improvements in my own life. Much as I would expect someone to use my blog for.

2. ***Researching topics of interest:*** I attempted to curate my social media feeds to topics I was interested in. I unfollowed everything except for a couple pages that featured topics I was truly interested in. However, the platforms filled my newsfeed with ads and suggested posts that took away from the ease of simply reading to learn. I now learn mainly from books (opting most times for audio versions), researching specific topics of interest on the world wide web, from others' experiences on Reddit, and, of course, from people in person via conversations.

How I Am Intentional with Social Media Use as a Friend and Family Member

1. ***Posting on my terms:*** In assessing my values, I know that I have a need to share. But I knew that I could achieve what I was looking to achieve with only a few platforms. I find it valuable to post to stories on Instagram and Facebook, for instance, thus making Snapchat sort of obsolete for me.

Posting to Instagram and Facebook is a one-and-done action. It takes little time, and it posts to both simultaneously. There is no editing needed. Sharing to "stories" is also a simple way to promote on my personal account that I am living out what I say I am living out. Sharing to a private Instagram account helps me keep my photos tidy, and reach a small number of loved ones. Writing is the creative venture I am pursuing, and this book is the sharing of that creativity. Though it feels uncomfortable to share what is essentially the personal contents of my journal, sharing in the format of a book feels less intimating than a regular blog.

2. ***Reciprocating in my own way:*** The ability to offer love and care is a strength of mine. This includes reciprocal relationships. I am willing to meet loved ones where they are at by looking through their photos. But this will be on my time, and it won't be mentioned with a like, but perhaps with a text or comment in person. It also means that if I don't find the time, it means reaching out to get together or to chat on the phone. Most importantly, looking through other's highlights online won't be done in the middle of movie time with my kids, or when I'm out on a date with my husband. Setting aside time to look through photos of my parents' travels, a friend's new baby, or whatever I may find valuable to see will be when the time is right.

3. *Meeting loved one's half way.* When meeting up with loved ones I don't see often, I discovered I was missing something. But in getting together with various family members on both sides of my family, who I admired, I found I could take some of what they were doing online to connect better with them. If communicating via technology was a spectrum, I discovered that being too far on the no-smart technology side was too far for me. It is why I am not interested in a "dumb" phone. Obviously, being too far on the all-in on smart technology was too much for me. I realized I had too many times gone all-in, thus forcing me to go too far out. For instance, when I found my text messaging app overcome with group chats, I stopped responding to them entirely, even those I should be communicating with regularly. In moving too far to the zero-tolerance end of the spectrum I was removing a use of technology that could actually add to my relationships. So, I reignited chats that matter to me and reduced my social communication down to the messaging apps that would allow me to have a regular presence with those few.

Overall, I am working to use any technology I have allowed in my life with clear and intentional purpose and leaving the rest in the dust. When I slip up, I give myself grace. I am committing to constantly experimenting and trying to find the screen-life balance that works for me and my family. I am unfollowing, deleting, and muting in order to block out the wrong stuff so I can focus on the right stuff. With the extra time it grants me, I am looking to make life feel so great, I simply forget about the screen.

Conclusion

How wonderful it is that nobody need wait a single moment before starting to improve the world.
—*Anne Frank*

I wrote this book as a way to share my process for developing a better way to coexist with technology and as a call to action. I've been a self-proclaimed analyzer my whole life. I spend a lot of time on self-development, and I am a natural observer of others. Through the years, I've noticed some unpleasant changes to society in general. Part of my role in education is to work on some of our school district's most challenging cases. I used to tell my spouse I feared the world was crumbling. He, a general education teacher, waved my worries off, attributing my fears to the unique situations I worked in. Now, he understands my concerns and see their validity. Like other educators today, he also comments on how things are changing. When I think back to my days working in customer service, I notice a vast difference from the way people used to talk to each other. When I was a restaurant server in the early 2000s, and a barista in the 2010s, communicating with strangers was pleasant. Being a customer service employee used to mean a requirement to treat customers with over-the-top, friendly service. Interacting with customers had its challenges, but it was also fun to interact with new people regularly. Today, it feels as though society has given up on thoughtful, service-oriented interaction. Many corporations have given up on enforcing standards, as if making customers happy is too challenging. Perhaps training people who are deficit in social skills due to excessive screen use is a lost cause. How has overall communication seemed to have gotten worse in the real world when one of technology's greatest contributions is the *improvement of communication?*

Despite my personal observations and theories, I remain hopeful we can turn this around. I want to encourage others to be intentional for both the purpose of simplifying, but also to help make this world a better place because of technology, not in spite of it. If we practice intentionality, we can again prioritize the world that we live and breathe in. Let's look to what actions, when it comes to technology, we can take to improve humanity instead of altering it for the worse. If like-minded individuals come together, we can gain strength in numbers. We can figure out how to coexist better with technology and help younger generations do so more easily. I challenge you to start by committing to going against the current, as strong as it is.

Unfollow

Just because everyone around you is doing something doesn't mean it's the best course of action for you. Let go of anything that's not serving you. Don't bring anything into your world in the first place unless it is within your value set. Don't follow others blindly. Don't settle for the status quo. Put people first. Build a community to strengthen your cause. Find strength in others who share your values. Don't let fear pressure you to take on more than you need to, or to forget your values altogether. What's the worst that can happen? You will be different than others? Forgotten? Rejected? Practice being okay with that.

Unplug

Commit to constantly experimenting without technology, and only allow back what works to improve your life. Stay curious. Be a lifelong learner. Figure out scaffolds and supports to put in place for you and your loved ones so that new habits stick. Take time to assess your values. Use them as a guide. Reset by taking regular breaks from different technologies. You might find that you have little interest to get back on. Experiment with technology as a tool for minimal, but truly authentic connection. Put your mental health first. Keep learning from others in the real world. Be a curious observer. Keep future generations in mind.

Demonstrate the use of "old-fashioned" ways. There are many apps out there to help you simplify your online experience, but try unplugging first. Think about what actions you can take outside of the screen first before using the screen as a solution. Look to spend most of your time and energy in the real world. Put your focus into practicing good health.

Unwind

Reap the benefits that come with intentional living. Let tech support you in your pursuit of living out your purpose but little more. Enjoy simple moments with others. Learn what it feels like to breathe deeply and live mindfully. Model to others what it could be like to enjoy moments instead of sighing and complaining. Remove before adding anything else. Spend time in nature, connect more with others—without a screen. Adopt simpler aspects from the past into your life. Worry less about who will judge you for being offline. Focus your energy on self-validation. Practice the joy of missing out on what is on the screen. You'll never know how much you might like it until you try it.

Notes

Preface: A Season of Clarity

1. **Definition of "unfollow," dictionary.com,**
   https://www.dictionary.com/browse/unfollow.

Introduction: "I Just Don't Like This Weirdo Aspect of the World"

1. Peter Attia, M.D., *Outlive: The Science and Art of* Longevity (Harmony 2023).

2. Drew Barrymore interview, **Elle** team editors, "18 Celebrities Who Have Called Out the Toxicity of Social Media," September 6, 2022,
   https://www.elle.com.au/life/health-wellness/13-celebrities-who-think-social-media-is-toxic-9829/.

Chapter 2: Unfollow Scrolling-Induced Depression

1. David D. Burns, *Feeling Good: Overcome Depression and Anxiety with Proven Techniques* (William Morrow & Co 1980).

2. Ibid.

3. Mel Robbins, *The High 5 Habit*: Take Control of Your Life with One Simple Habit (Hay House Inc., 2021).

Chapter 6: Unfollow Refusing to Embrace Discomfort

1. Lynam I, Catley D, Goggin K, Rabinowitz JL, Gerkovich MM, Williams K, Wright J; MOTIV8. *"Autonomous regulation and locus of control as predictors of antiretroviral medication adherence."* J Health Psychol. 2009 May;14(4):578–86. doi: 10.1177/1359105309103577. PMID: 19383658; PMCID: PMC2733914.

2. Kesavayuth D, Binh Tran D, Zikos V. *"Locus of control and subjective well-being: Panel evidence from Australia."* PLoS One. 2022 Aug 31;17(8):e0272714. doi: 10.1371/journal.pone.0272714. PMID: 36044403; PMCID: PMC9432765.

3. Nicholas Kardaras, *Glow Kids: How Screen Addiction Is Hijacking Our Kids-And How to Break the Trance* (St. Martin's Press 2016).

Chapter 7: Unfollow Your Bad Tech Habits

1. Anna Lembke, *Dopamine Nation: Finding Balance in the Age of Indulgence* (Dutton 2021).

Chapter 8: Unfollow Bad Influencers

1. Edward Sri, *The Art of Living: The Cardinal Virtues and the Freedom to Love* (Augustine Institute – Ignatius Press 2021).
2. Josh Fields Milburn, *The Minimalists Podcast.*

Chapter 12: Unfollow Creativity Inhibitors

1. Eve Rodsky, *Fair Game: A Game-Changing Solution for When You Have Too Much to Do (and More Life to Live)* (G.P. Putnam's Sons 2021).

Chapter 15: Unfollow Risky Behavior

1. Bowman, Katy. *Rethink Your Position: Reshape Your Exercise, Yoga, and Everyday Movement, One Part at a Time.* (Propriometrics Press, 2023).

2. Lee, Eun Jee PhD, RN; Ogbolu, Yolanda PhD, CRNP-Neonatal, FNAP. *Does Parental Control Work With Smartphone Addiction?: A Cross-Sectional Study of Children in South Korea.* Journal of Addictions Nursing 29(2):p 128-138, 4/6 2018. | DOI: 10.1097/JAN.0000000000000222.

Chapter 17: Unfollow Irresponsible Parenting

1. Georgia Wells, Jeff Horowitz, and Depa Seetharaman, "Facebook knows Instagram is harmful for teens, its own documents show," Wall Street Journal, September 14, 2021, https://www.wsj.com/tech/personal-tech/facebook-knows-instagram-is-toxic-for-teen-girls-company-documents-show-11631620739?mod=hp_lead_pos7.

2. Ibid.

3. Ibid.

4. Ibid.

5. Ibid.

Chapter 21: Commitment to Continuous Experimentation

1. David D. Burns, *Ten Days to Self-Esteem (William Morrow Paperbacks 1999).*

2. Linda Peckel, "6 behavioral criteria that had the highest diagnostic accuracy for the diagnosis of smartphone addiction," Psychiatry Advisor, July 27, 2017, https://www.psychiatryadvisor.com/features/criteria-for-identification-of-smartphone-addiction/.

3. Ibid.

About the Author

Emily Feldpausch is a special education teacher and co-owner of High Five Fitness of Williamston, which she runs alongside her husband, Nathan. She holds a Master of Arts in Teaching, a Master of Arts in Special Education, a Bachelor of Arts in Psychology, and a CrossFit Level 1 Trainer certification. She coaches adult strength training and youth sports, blending education, movement, and mindset to support whole-person well-being.

A personal experiment with social media sparked Feldpausch's curiosity about its effects on mental health, leading her to explore healthier, more intentional ways of coexisting with technology. What began as a blog evolved into a deeper examination of how habits, mindset, and movement shape everyday life and long-term well-being.

Through her teaching, fitness business, and writing, Feldpausch is passionate about encouraging both mental and physical health. She practices what she writes by maintaining a minimal and intentional presence on social media, believing that meaningful change begins with awareness, self-compassion, and small, sustainable choices.

Her personal interests include singing, visual art, spirituality, and spending time with her husband and their three active sons.

To connect with Emily and access resources referenced in the book, visit **www.emilyfeldpausch.com**

www.highfivefitnesswilliamston.com